CHILDREN OF JONESTOWN

Kenneth Wooden

McGRAW-HILL BOOK COMPANY
New York   St. Louis   San Francisco
Bogotá   Guatemala   Hamburg
Mexico   Montreal   Panama   Paris
São Paulo   Tokyo   Toronto

Copyright © 1981 by Kenneth Wooden.

All rights reserved. Printed in the United States of America. No part of this book may be reproduced, stored in a retrieval system or transmitted in any form or by any means, electronic, mechanical, photocopying, recording or otherwise, without the prior written permission of the publisher.

First McGraw-Hill Paperback edition

2 3 4 5 6 7 8 9 10 11   BKP BKP   8 9 8 7 6 5

Library of Congress Cataloging in Publication Data

Wooden, Kenneth
The children of Jonestown.

Bibliography: p.
1. Peoples Temple.   2. Children—Guyana.
3. Children—United States.   I. Title
BP605.P46W66   362.7′044   80-16663
ISBN 0-07-071641-2 (pbk.)

Each second we live is a new and unique moment of the universe, a moment that never was before and never will be again. And what do we teach our children in school? We teach them that two and two make four and that Paris is the capital of France. When will we also teach them what they are? We should say to each of them: Do you know what you are? You are a marvel. You are unique. In all of the world there is no other child exactly like you. In the millions of years that have passed, there has never been a child like you. And look at your body—what a wonder it is! Your legs, your arms, your cunning fingers, the way you move! You may become a Shakespeare, a Michelangelo, a Beethoven. You have the capacity for anything. Yes, you are a marvel.

And when you grow up, can you then harm another who is, like you, a marvel? You must cherish one another. You must work—we all must work—to make this world worthy of its children.

Pablo Casals

TO

GRACE THERESA WARD

EDWARD FRANKLIN WOODEN

MADELINE AGNES WEAKLAND

FRANK JOHN BRAUN

My loving mother and father and the good, hardworking parents of my wife, Martha B. Braun, for keeping our families together in times of severe personal trials—illness, the Depression, and war—and for the love, protection, and responsibility they gave to us as children. Because of their sacrifices and values, hopefully we of another generation can ward off the modern forces of disunity that threaten all families, and in so doing, strengthen our own children to face the challenges of their time.

To all families the world over, including those of my stepmother, Effie Spencer, who continue to pass on proven and age-old values of family life.

To mothers and fathers all, especially those whose children are trapped in authoritarian and dishonest cults, I dedicate this book from broken dreams and heartaches of the destroyed families of Jonestown, with the hope that it will never happen again.

Acknowledgments

Without the vision and unique sensitivity of Stuart Loorey, managing editor of the *Chicago Sun-Times,* and the close assistance of fellow reporter Bill Braden, this story, originally planned for *NBC News,* might never have been brought to light. By giving it the importance it deserved, the *Sun-Times* gave the children of Jonestown some of the dignity they were denied. I am proud to be associated with such an outstanding newspaper and am forever grateful for its assistance, especially in sending me to Guyana.

Two NBC producers were of tremendous assistance in the early stages of my investigative reporting: Clare Crawford Mason and Janet Janjigan. Clare and Janet exhibited a sense of responsibility that went beyond news gathering; both still believe in the story.

My thanks also to Edward Planer, NBC News Vice President, for graciously permitting the use of illustrations from films shot by NBC News at Jonestown hours before the massacre.

Marie White of the Citizen's Advocates in Sacramento, California, was an invaluable source of help and information, as was an old friend, George Jacobs of American Polymers, Inc., who kept my phone line open when financial resources were running low and who provided a key lead for obtaining information.

As I drafted this acknowledgment, I heard the sad and

chilling news that three close friends and ex-Temple members, Al and Jeannie Mills and their daughter, Daphne, were murdered in their home in Berkeley, California. The Mills family was extremely helpful to me when I first visited San Francisco in February 1979 to begin work on *The Children of Jonestown*. As a fellow author (*Six Years with God*), Jeannie shared documents and advice out of a ministerial zeal to educate the American public on the menace of cults. And when I lost an important document about celebrities and others who allegedly supported Jim Jones, Jeannie kindly and graciously understood. Daphne was just beginning to enjoy life after the traumatic effects of living in People's Temple, of being threatened daily after defecting, and, finally, of coping with the deaths of all her childhood friends. The Millses were a courageous family who would not let fear rule their lives.

There are people I wish I could publicly thank, people who cared deeply about the children about whom I have written and who extended themselves to the point of putting their jobs in jeopardy at times. They know who they are, both in Guyana and in the United States. This book would also have been impossible without their compassionate outrage and the documented information which they provided.

Many thanks to Tim Yohn and Tom Dembofsky of McGraw-Hill, who saw the importance of this book and gave me their vote of confidence. A special note of appreciation, too, to Ed and Linda Struzik, who transcribed a lengthy taped interview to lighten my work load.

To my teen-age daughters—Grace, Rosemary, and Jennifer—whom I neglected totally but kept running into at the kitchen stove as we all made endless cups of tea—they at their schoolwork, my wife and I at work on this book—I convey my appreciation of their understanding during some trying moments.

Without my wife, Martha, who not only edited the first drafts and typed the entire manuscript but also challenged endless points for clarity, this book would only be a distant dream.

And finally, I thank my eight-year-old son, John Allen, who helped me with some spelling. John built forts and airports around my feet and left notes on my desk about little things: "Dad, I fell out of the attic." . . . "When can we play chess . . . war . . . watch *M.A.S.H.*?"—all of which spelled love and "don't forget me." John was a constant reminder of the children I was writing about with much melancholy, for I knew they never had a chance to play in the same garden of childhood.

June 1980
Bucks County, Pennsylvania

Contents

Prologue   1
1. Child Abuse and Terror in People's Temple   6
2. Manipulation of Court Guardianships and Children's Lives   20
3. Jim Jones Versus the Family   38
4. Brainwashing Dreams   57
5. Financial Building Blocks of Jones' Empire   76
6. Politics + Public Relations = Power   91
7. The Paralysis and Failure of Government   116
8. The Quest of Leo Ryan   146
9. The Last White Night   171
10. The Politics of National Shame   192
11. The Cults and Human Rights for Children   202
Appendix: "Accusation of Human Rights Violations by Rev. James Warren Jones Against Our Children and Relatives . . ." by the Concerned Relatives Organization, April 11, 1978.   210
Bibliography and Sources   221
Index   229

> "Do not fear your enemies: The worst they can do is kill you. Do not fear friends: At worst they may betray you. Fear those who do not care: They neither kill nor betray, but betrayal and murder exist because of their silent consent."
>
> Bruno Yasensky, Russian novelist

Prologue

On November 18, 1978, virtually on the eve of the International Year of the Child, 276 children were murdered in an unprecedented act of cult genocide in Jonestown, Guyana. The imposed silence that followed their brutal deaths cast a long shadow on the sincerity of this country's 1979 commitment to the International Year of the Child. Totally ignored by President Jimmy Carter, Governor Jerry Brown, and other national leaders and lost in all the national and international press coverage on the tragedy, they were buried in unmarked, bulldozed, common graves in Oakland, California. Both the White House and the State Department were more than anxious to put the Jonestown matter to rest, and officials responsible for the bodies until interment were ordered to keep the lowest possible public profile. So it is that these children, insignificant hostages in life, have all but been forgotten in death.

On April 14, 1978, seven months before the mass murders of these innocent children, President Carter announced the establishment of the United States Commission on the International Year of the Child for 1979 by Executive Order 12053:

> We shall foster within the United States a better understanding of the special needs of children. In particular . . . special attention to the health, education, social environment, physical and emotional development, and legal rights and needs of children that are unique to them as children.

On June 8, 1978, Carter made an even stronger commitment to the Commission when he said, "I hope to add the prestige and influence of the Presidency itself to making this a successful effort."

As this book was written, nearly fifty American citizens were being held hostage in the U.S. Embassy in Teheran, Iran. When Iranian militants seized the Embassy and took hostages, President Carter and Secretary of State Cyrus Vance spoke out strongly against this violation of international law as well as against the conditions that the hostages were forced to endure. Our nation responded with a massive wave of heartfelt concern and patriotism.

Yet only a little over a year before, a group of Concerned Relatives submitted a moving and well-documented petition to Secretary Vance, entreating him to protect the human rights of loved ones being held by Jim Jones in a jungle encampment in Guyana, South America. Defectors from Jonestown told, in sworn affidavits, of over 1,000 people imprisoned, of armed guards preventing their escape, and of the deadly threat of "revolutionary suicide/murder" at the hands of their isolated and mad leader.

When a shocked nation was informed that all the Jonestown hostages were dead, the President expressed sorrow to the immediate families of the murdered press corps and Congressman Leo Ryan. Not until almost two weeks later did Mr. Carter finally comment on what happened at Jonestown itself. During a nationally televised news conference, he stated, ". . . I believe that we don't need to deplore on a nationwide basis the fact that the Jonestown cult, so called, was typical of America, because it is not" and stressed, "It did not take place in our country."

What the President ignored was the fact that although the deaths did not occur on our soil, those 276 babies, toddlers, youngsters, and teen-agers came from every corner of the United States: Chicago, Miami, Indianapolis, Atlanta, Los Angeles, Philadelphia, Detroit, Omaha, San Francisco, Kansas City, Houston, New Orleans, Springfield (Ohio), Trenton, Little Rock, Denver, Jackson (Mississippi), and a host of smaller cities and rural towns.

It matters little where these children perished. What matters is why they died in the manner they did. Other major human disasters or near-disasters have been investigated by either a Presidential commission or an in-depth inquiry by an appropriate federal agency—the DC10 crash in Chicago, May 1979, and the Three Mile Island incident, for example. To date, the Jonestown tragedy has not been given the national priority or attention it deserves.

Authorities did conduct three routine investigations, with little fanfare: No one was found responsible. Moreover, U.S. Attorney General Griffin Bell refused to release to people interested in further study the murder/suicide tapes found at Jonestown, on the grounds that they served "no purpose." Bell admitted that he had not listened to the tapes, saying, "I do not suffer from morbid curiosity. It is not one of my traits . . . Jonestown was an aberration that is not likely to occur again."

But was it an aberration? In view of estimates that three to ten million Americans are trapped in cults that employ the same oppressive and dishonest techniques as Jim Jones' People's Temple, how can we be certain it will never happen again? There is a growing cry for help from those who have already lost their loved ones to cults, and they feel their pleas are being ignored. Can we as a free people afford to tolerate apathy and silence on the part of authorities?

The International Year of the Child has passed, and the silence on the factors that led to the mass slaughter of the children of Jonestown endures. The apathy of those responsible at all levels of government before the tragedy turned into imposed official silence after it. Without question, the President set the national tone.

In 1979, President Carter created a Commission on the Holocaust, which addressed itself to the eleven million Jewish and other victims of Nazi genocide during World War II. To Commission Chairman Elie Wiesel and his colleagues, the President said, "Never again will the world stand silent or look the other way in the face of genocide. We must stamp out oppression wherever it exists." With that, he urged the founding of a museum, a memorial, and an educational foundation, as well as the establishment of a Committee of Conscience for the purpose of receiving reports of any new attempts at genocide.

It appears that the unique problem facing the children

of Jonestown was the total lack of a powerful lobbying group to represent them in Washington and Sacramento. As a result, their President, their Governor—all of government—did not care enough to look down and see their sad and horrible plight. Children don't vote; hence, consciously or unconsciously, they were cast aside in the priority process of political power. They had only their loved ones and a lone public official, the late Congressman Leo Ryan, who could not succeed in the savage battle to save them.

Time moves on. Let this book record, however, that during the final moments in the lives of hundreds trapped in a concentration camp in Jonestown, Guyana, there was betrayal and murder because those who could have helped chose to give, instead, their silent consent.

> "Children who said they were not happy and wanted to go away were severely beaten."
>
> Tracy Parks, aged ten, who escaped the massacre but whose mother died at Port Kaituma, Guyana

1. Child Abuse and Terror in People's Temple

The 276 children who died in Jonestown were hostages of an insane terrorist who cruelly abused them and finally murdered them to win a place in history. From the time they entered People's Temple with their parents till they were killed with cyanide poison in Guyana, Reverend Jim Jones manipulated them to create a favorable media image, to win the support of celebrities and political leaders, and to enrich the Temple's coffers with public money. Through them he was able to keep their parents in his church, to obtain all their possessions and savings, and to lure these innocent believers to Guyana, where they lost their freedom and, ultimately, their lives.

On the day that Congressman Leo Ryan and his party of Concerned Relatives and working press were expected to arrive at Jonestown, Jim Jones' voice blared from the loudspeakers in the compound: "If you mess up, you will get the severest punishment!" The children, as well as everyone else, knew that the big man with dark glasses was not fooling. To varying degrees they understood all too well the potential horror that awaited them in what was called "life in an experimental community," but was in reality a brutal and sadistic concentration camp.

Five-year-old Tracy Arterberry was punished for being restless in class. Blindfolded at night and taken to a well approximately one-quarter of a mile from the main pavilion, she was told that monsters and snakes were waiting for her at the 14-foot well. As she approached the area, a slimy rope—a "snake"—was placed on her bare shoulders, while adults, hidden nearby, made monster sounds. Tracy's screaming was heard back at the camp. It continued long after she was put to bed.

Eleven-year-old Nawab Lawrence also had a slight discipline problem in class. He, too, was taken to the well, a rope was placed under his arms, and he was thrown in. Adult "monsters" in the well pulled and yanked at his arms, legs, and head as he violently splashed and screamed in terror. One People's Temple member recalled:

> You could hear the child screaming all the way there and all the way back, "I'm sorry, I'm sorry, Father! I'm sorry, Father!" And if he didn't scream loud enough how sorry he was, then Jones would send the child back down.

Michele Brady, twelve, a child under a California state guardianship, had a history of mental instability and was often abused because she couldn't control her actions at the camp. Michele was put in a plywood box 3 feet wide, 6 feet long, and 4 feet high, with two fender holes that admitted air but no light. Kept there for weeks with nothing but a can for toilet, she was taunted constantly by passersby.

Tommy Bogue and Jerry Wilson, both seventeen, were beaten for minor reasons such as resting at work without permission and disagreeing on seed yield and amounts of fertilizer to be used on the crops. Wilson had his teeth knocked out during a public beating. Bogue was subjected to "stretching" by four security guards, each of whom grabbed a limb and pulled it until he was unconscious; his father feared he would die.

Of the above, only Tommy Bogue survived, though he was wounded at the airstrip when Congressman Ryan and the others were killed. According to the Bogue family, and confirmed by members of the Jonestown basketball team who escaped the mass murders/suicides, other forms of punishment for both adults and children included:

- Digging a 9 by 9 by 9-foot hole and filling it up again, which took around thirty hours, unless it rained, when it took longer, because water had to be bailed to prevent mud slides and drowning.
- Confinement in the cellar, which was 90 feet long, 12 feet wide, and 10 to 12 feet deep.
- Hard labor, called "public service," for people six years old and up. They were confined to cottage #11, crowded like cattle in an area with almost no open floor space. Later, observers on the scene dubbed it "slave ship."

- Beatings by security guards and other high-ranking members, including Jones' own son, Steven, while Jones sat in his throne chair, supervising and encouraging the assaulters.

There was little to eat and little time to sleep in Jonestown. The workday began at 7 A.M. and lasted till 6 P.M. There was a one-hour lunch break, much of which was spent standing in line for rice soup, gravy, and greens. One survivor recalled, "Since complaints about the food were dealt with severely, little was said about the maggots in the rice. Either you picked them out while sitting in the light, or, if you were too weary from long work in the fields, you just ate them." Jones, however, dined on eggs, chicken, pork, canned fruits, vegetables, soda, cake, and candy, and drank cognac. (Once a week he would pass out one cookie per person, but only to those who had been "good"—a practice later stopped during an economy drive.) By 7 P.M., the long meetings and public punishments would commence, and Jones would harangue far into the night.

The realities of People's Temple were very different from its pretentious propaganda. During the mid-1970s, People's Temple Choir buses roamed the country. Many newspapers recorded the smiling faces and good works of the children. A *Washington Post* editorial commented:

> The hands-down winners of anybody's tourists-of-the-year award have got to be the 660 wonderful members of the People's Temple Christian Church of Redwood Valley, California, who bend over backwards to leave every place they visit more attractive than when they arrived. Like thousands of other tourists, they went calling on the U.S. Capitol the other day; but unlike others who tramp through our town spreading litter helter-skelter, this spirited group of travelers fanned out from their 13

buses and spent an hour cleaning up the grounds. . . . The church . . . has already won friends in dozens of cities since its tour left Redwood Valley August 8, and still more areas will benefit by the members' stopoffs on their return trip.

The *Post* and other newspapers across the country that commented favorably on the tour didn't know that these "spirited" children were carried like baggage on the thirteen buses, in overhead racks, on the floors, even in the luggage compartments, except in the spacious bus that housed Jim Jones and his inner circle. The vehicles smelled bad since, to make time, they rarely stopped for passengers to use restrooms. They had to make do with open cans on the buses. As the late former Temple member Jeannie Mills recalled in her book, *Six Years with God,* "Toilet paper was rationed out because Jones feared we wasted it. One piece for #1 and two pieces for #2." For a period of time when they did stop at public facilities, "counselors were stationed in the toilet stalls to hand out paper."

The traveling took a heavy toll on the children as well as on the adults. No one had time to sleep properly on a typical weekend, when Temple members would go south from their Redwood, California, retreat en masse for services in San Francisco and L.A. The buses rolled into San Francisco for Saturday-evening services. Immediately after, they traveled all night to Los Angeles, arriving by noon on Sunday. After Sunday worship, the buses drove north the entire night, arriving back in Redwood on Monday at 6:30 A.M., in time for the children to catch school buses for another hour-and-a-half trip. Ruby Bogner, a teacher at Redwood School, recalled that the children were so tired, they would fall asleep and sleep right through classes. "I would feel so sorry for them," she said, "that I would take their jackets and sweaters and cover their heads and shoulders and permit them to get the sleep they needed."

Once Jones made a record with the title *HE'S ABLE— People's Temple Choir,* which starts with a lovely, lively song, "Welcome," sung by youngsters of between two and seven years old. "He keeps me singing a happy song; he keeps me singing it all day long . . ." the song goes in part. In fact, the children had to stay in a recording studio more than fourteen hours straight, until the song was recorded correctly.

Physical abuse of the young was part of the routine at People's Temple. As Jones began to exercise total control, children were beaten if they failed to call him Father or were otherwise disrespectful, or if they talked with peers who were not members of People's Temple. Belts were used at first, then were replaced by elm switches, which in turn were replaced by the "board of education," a long, hard piece of wood, swung by 250-pound Ruby Carroll. According to Grace Stoen, wife of a Temple lawyer, and a counselor until her defection in 1976, the children were faced with punishments that escalated in terms of severity:

> Mild discipline gave way to making young girls strip almost nude in front of the full membership and then forcing them to take cold showers or jump into the cold swimming pool at the Redwood Valley Church. Unequal boxing matches gave way to beatings with paddles, then electric shock, and finally something [Jones] called "a blue-eyed monster," which hurt and terrorized the younger ones in a darkened room.

A five-year-old described in incoherent detail his experience with Jones' monster:

> . . . them people made me lay down on a big chair, you know . . . These cut, these knives that comes down and

cuts your shirt open and your stomach . . . my stomach was tore open, remember? . . . They cutted your bone open—they went all the way down to your bone. That hurts. They had something come out of the blue-eyed monster . . . they were going to eat me up. Yeah, that shocks you, you know, shaking like this . . .

A monster drawing by one of the children that may have been inspired by such an experience was found in the San Francisco Temple building.

Jones rarely hit anyone himself. As a rule, he simply sat and laughed hysterically as big Ruby Carroll's "board of education" delivered between one and two hundred strokes to children and adults. However, on one occasion Grace Stoen saw Jones "beat a young boy with a wet rubber hose so hard, the boy had to have his penis cauterized to stop the bleeding." He once confided to Jeannie Mills that it excited him sexually to hear youngsters crying in pain and that one boy in particular aroused him. A few days later, on a small pretext, that boy was beaten severely.

In another incident, when a young girl tenderly approached a shaken friend who has just received 150 whacks from the "board of education," Grace Stoen overheard this as the girl was reprimanded by Jones: "Get the hell away from him. . . . I should put acid in your cunt."

By the time the Temple buildings were wired for sound and speakers were placed throughout, the nightmare was total. As late as two or three in the morning, youngsters were awakened and taken into "planning commission" meetings for beatings. A microphone was held to their mouths so that everyone could hear their screams, mingled with the laughter of Jim Jones.

Perhaps the most frightening aspect of this abuse is that much of it was done legally and the rest covered up by Jones' extensive political influence. Parents or guardians of children under eighteen were forced to sign a notarized release, prepared by Temple lawyers, that gave Jones legal permission to punish and terrorize their children or wards.

On October 6, 1975, a Ukiah school counselor, Darwin Richardson, filed a child abuse petition against Jack Beam, one of Jones' top lieutenants, for the beating of his own son, Anthony, using an extension cord folded in half four times, one end taped for a handle, with the loops on the other end cut and the insulation peeled back to leave the wires bare. The Richardson report was filed at 9:30 A.M., but because Jones had Temple members placed in jobs in the human services departments of the county, within four hours he had called everyone concerned with the issue and had the report killed.

Jim Jones, with his political influence, flouted with impunity the California Child Abuse Law, Title 22, which states, ". . . children cannot be subject to verbal or physical abuse, are entitled to the right of religion and must be treated with dignity." But not even this token protection was available in Jonestown, where the leader was the law and tyranny flourished.

Before departing for Guyana, all members had to fill out the Temple's Form 10, "Promised Land Work Preference." The forms found after the massacre show that few children had any experience or willingness to work in construction, agriculture, or other heavy industry. Yet roughly 60 percent of the 100 or more people who were on continuous hard labor were teen-agers. Also earmarked for "public service" were many of the young people in school who were bored with the poor education and its heavy doses of Soviet propaganda films and Communist Chinese booklets, such as *Lin Wen Hsuen: A Boy Martyr*. Those who didn't work hard enough at "public service" received isolation in wooden boxes, an idea of Tom Grubbs, the school principal. Juanita Bogue described it this way: "We'd work in temperatures as high as 120 degrees all day with only a ten-minute break . . . If you stopped to rest and leaned on your hoe, the security forces would write down the time wasted." Juanita's outspoken and independent older brother, Tommy, was constantly punished by Jones. On one occasion, his legs were "put in chains" so that he would be unable to leave the settlement but could still work in the fields. Those who succeeded in getting away from the compound were almost always caught and heavily drugged.

All incoming and outgoing mail was censored and all were told what to write in their letters. Janet Tupper, who would soon unwittingly commit suicide, wrote her father, Lawrence:

> We are as happy as one could possibly be! We saw all the dirty old articles in *The Progress* [a small San Francisco newspaper] that you put in, and we didn't like it. This is a beautiful place so just quit bothering us. Sincerely yours truly.

At one meal, Juanita Bogue reported, Jones told the children that they had just eaten a dead man. Youngsters were forced to eat hot peppers and their own vomit, and toddlers who soiled their underclothes were made to wear the fouled clothing on their heads. Jones raged over a little boy's killing a bug. Once he ordered the collection and destruction of all the dolls because "a curse was put on [his] life." To prevent the youngsters from constantly running around the compound, he claimed there weren't enough shoes to go around because the "federal customs agents broke into a shipment of children's shoes and stole them." Toddlers were confined to a fenced-in dirt playground, where fifty of them played in an area 6 by 10 feet. According to one escapee's account in the summer before the massacre:

> They're all sick. All the children have ringworm or some kind of little parasite. A lot of them have their hair missing in various places and oozing sores on their legs. There is very little medication given to them and they mainly use cassava powder to put on the sores. It doesn't do any good.

Jones' sexual exploitation of his adult followers has been documented, but little has been said about the sexual abuse of the children of People's Temple. According to information pieced together from church members in San Francisco and Jonestown and from a Guyanese official who lived in Mabaruma, a town eighty miles northeast of Jonestown, the children were subject to constant sexual molestation. In California, teen-age girls were forced into prostitution to pleasure influential persons who Jones felt could enhance his political power. "Black-(fe)mailing them" was Jones' ribald label for it. While he usually used girls over eighteen years of age, reliable sources have corroborated an incident in which he purposely sent two fifteen-year-olds to service a prominent Californian. He later told the man that a mistake had been made, and "now [Jones] was having a difficult time keeping the girls' parents in line."

An adult Temple member with a long history of sexually assaulting children was assigned to work with the youngsters. Caught raping a ten-year-old boy, the man was beaten in front of the Temple's assembled membership, then shipped back to work again with the same children.

In San Francisco, Jones raped a fifteen-year-old boy and forced him into a homosexual relationship that continued until Jones left permanently for Guyana. The youth miraculously escaped going to Jonestown. He still lives in the Bay Area but suffers greatly from the trauma of the experience, especially since the massacre.

At one point, a Guyanese official heard about the sexual goings-on involving children, which sounded so bizarre to him that he did not believe what he heard. If husbands and wives were caught talking privately, it was their children who were punished. In these cases, daughters were forced to masturbate in public or to have sex with someone they didn't like before the entire Jonestown population, children as well as adults.

At the same time, Jones became increasingly dependent on drugs; more and more paranoid, he had longer, more frequent periods of crazed irresponsibility. Concerned ex-Temple members had begun monitoring the radio messages between Guyana and church members in San Francisco, and noted that large quantities of Thorazine were being ordered for the jungle settlement. As Jones' paranoia and his own dependency on drugs reached monstrous proportions, he unleashed them on his faithful. Not only had he restrained them psychologically and physically, but now, unknown to them, he began to give them powerful mind-controlling pills. After the deaths, huge quantities of drugs were found at Jonestown: well over 11,000 doses of Thorazine, along with massive amounts of Quaalude, Demerol, Valium, and morphine.

According to Dr. C. Leslie Mootoo, chief medical examiner of Guyana, there were more drugs in Jonestown (where the population was never more than 1,000) than were needed or could ever be used legally by the 66,000 inhabitants of Georgetown, the capital of Guyana. While the drugs were used primarily to calm down the Jonestown residents, they were increasingly employed for purposes of punishment, intimidation, and control. In

September 1977, they were given to the children of Jonestown in what is now believed to be the leader's first serious attempt at carrying out his experiment with mass "suicide."

Dr. Joyce H. Lowinson, a member of President Carter's Strategy Council on Drug Abuse Prevention, told *The New York Times* that the drugs found at Jonestown indicated "either there were a lot of psychotic patients or they were using it to control people." Dale Parks, a nursing supervisor who left with Congressman Ryan, said:

> If a person wanted to leave Jonestown or if there was a breach of rules, one was taken to the extended-care unit. It was a rehabilitation place where one would be reintegrated back into the community. The people were given drugs to keep them under control.

Another survivor told about a young teen-ager who attempted to escape and was caught. The youth was placed in solitary confinement and drugged for about a week. When he was let out, his face was completely distorted from massive doses of Thorazine and Quaalude. Jones, however, told everyone that the boy was a good example of what the jungle can do to you.

Charles Touchette, whose wife was totally devoted to Jones and would later, as a nurse, dispense the deadly cyanide to the youngsters, told this author in Guyana that there was a time he talked about leaving and taking his large family with him. Then be began to have what he thought was a series of small strokes, because he couldn't stay awake for any length of time. After the tragedy, Jones' natural son, Steven, told Touchette that his father had ordered that he be drugged. Jones feared an exodus of the Touchettes would give rise to an exit mentality.

By the summer of 1978, Jones was so addicted to amphetamine that Dr. Carlton Goodlett, his personal physican, told Temple lawyer Charles Garry that "Jones is literally burning his brains out with drugs."

A custody battle between Jones and Tim and Grace Stoen over their son, John Victor, whom Jones claimed to have sired, had been coming to a head. The courts of California and Guyana sided with the Stoens and instructed Jones to surrender the child, whom he was holding in Jonestown. A sworn statement by Deborah Blakey, a former high official of the People's Temple, dated June 15, 1978, conveyed the seriousness of the situation:

> The September 1977 crisis concerning John Stoen reached major proportions. The radio messages from Guyana were frenzied and hysterical. One morning, Terri J. Buford, public relations adviser to Rev. Jones, and myself were instructed to place a telephone call to a high-ranking Guyanese official who was visiting the United States and deliver the following threat. Unless the government of Guyana took immediate steps to stall the Guyanese court action regarding John Stoen's custody, the entire population of Jonestown would extinguish itself in a mass suicide by 5:30 P.M. that day. I was later informed that Temple members in Guyana placed similar calls to other Guyanese officials.... We later received radio communication to the effect that the court case had been stalled and that the suicide threat was called off.

In fact, Jones had decided to burn the members of his church to death in a warehouse. He came so close to carrying this out that "all of the babies had been given small doses of sleeping pills that day so that it would be easier for them to die."

Forced labor, hunger, corporal punishment, humiliation, drugging, and sexual abuse were insufficient to satiate the insane needs of Jones. He now sought the ultimate perverse fulfillment. Mass suicide rehearsals known as "White Nights" became part of the Jonestown routine, and talk of death the daily fare of the children. Shortly before the end, Jones conducted a three-day marathon of brainwashing and propaganda. He asked rhetorically, "Would you kill your child?" answering himself, "You would if you loved him enough." Then he asked, "How would you kill your child?" He was pleased by the assortment of answers, some of which were extremely violent, but said, "Well, I wouldn't kill them that way. I would do it gently, with a sedative. Just put them to sleep."

On another occasion, Jones again asked how they should kill their children. According to a survivor, Michael Touchette, someone gave a long, bloody, historical account of how one group did it by cutting off heads. A morbid discussion ensued, detailing a mass suicide for the adults "after they had cut off the heads of all the children." That night most of the children couldn't sleep for fear of finding in the morning that their heads had been cut off. The next day a delegation of older youths went to Jones, told him how upset the younger children were, and asked if they, too, couldn't be poisoned rather than decapitated. Jones smiled and said that Dr. Larry Schacht, the Jonestown physician, was looking into that possibility for everyone.

One teen-ager, still very upset, summed it up later in the day when he said to Juanita Bogue, "Jones only wants to make a name for himself. He doesn't give a shit about us. He only wants to use us to get into history."

> *"If parents gave up their child in guardianship to another person, and then they were to defect from the church, they wouldn't be able to get their child back without a big legal hassle; and, of course, with the amount of money Jim had and the attorneys he had, a young mother would feel absolutely helpless trying to fight it. . . .*
>
> *"Jim felt it was so important to get the legal guardianships for children . . . in case he ever wanted to take them down to Jonestown, he'd be able to get the papers he needed."*
>
> From an interview with Jeannie Mills, author of
> Six Years with God

2. Manipulation of Court Guardianships and Children's Lives

The deaths of 913 people of Jonestown are often described as "mass suicide," especially in governmental circles. However, more than one-quarter of the settlement's population were children ranging from infants born in Guyana to those at the age of consent. "Legally, under English law, a child cannot consent to suicide," said Cecil A. Roberts, deputy police commissioner of Guyana, a former British colony; ". . . all 276 were murdered."

To begin with, the children were not in Jonestown by educated choice. In the first major exodus from the

United States in the late spring and early summer of 1977, they were abruptly put on buses and transported to airports on the East Coast. They had no prior knowledge of arrangements. They all thought they were going off on a vacation. Instead, they became prisoners and eventual fatalities. But many would not have died if they had not been in the legal custody of Jim Jones under court-approved guardianships.

Jones brilliantly manipulated the law and the courts to gain control over the children of People's Temple, making it virtually impossible for them or their parents to break away. Careful research had convinced him that legal guardianships would provide the leverage he needed to keep children and adults in check. They would also provide a steady flow of cash to the church coffers. The plan was so successful that even after the tragedy, the investigation by the General Accounting Office of the Congress concluded that "Jones broke no laws in doing what he did."

Forty-five sets of court-approved guardianship papers, representing fifty-six young wards, were found in the files of People's Temple on Geary Street in San Francisco. (More are believed to exist, but the GAO was unable to confirm this during investigations because "California court officials were not very cooperative on the question.") These guardianships were processed through the superior courts—twenty-eight in the county of San Francisco, thirteen in Los Angeles County, ten in Mendocino County, four in Contra Costa County, and one in Alameda County—where unsupervised procedure permitted Jones to snare the children from their natural parents.

Children under California court guardianships who were taken to Guyana illegally are listed below by counties:

THE CHILDREN OF JONESTOWN

NAME	COURT CASE NO.	COUNTY COURT
Brown, Delaine Y.	47251	Contra Costa
Brown, Amanda D.	47251	Contra Costa
Brown, Jerross K.	47251	Contra Costa
Lopez, Vincent, Jr.	204 108 7	Alameda
Dover, Vicky	P 602822	Los Angeles
Green, Anita	608616	Los Angeles
LaMothe, Ramona	??	Los Angeles
Mitchell, Cheryl	P 597989	Los Angeles
Reed, Kenneth	P 597989	Los Angeles
Sellers, Marvin	P 615645	Los Angeles
Wilson, Jerry	P 618615	Los Angeles
Wright, Stanley	618614	Los Angeles
Anderson, Jerome	??	Mendocino
Brady, Michele	15515	Mendocino
Brady, Georgiann	15515	Mendocino
Buckley, Christopher	16320	Mendocino
Buckley, Dorothy	15711	Mendocino
Gardner, John Lawrence	14638	Mendocino
Runnels, Julie Ann	15959	Mendocino
Truss, Cornelius Lee	16288	Mendocino
Buckley, Frances E.	210463	San Francisco
Buckley, Odesta	210463	San Francisco
Campbell, Ronald	213013	San Francisco
Carroll, Randall E.	213015	San Francisco
Carroll, Rondell J.	213015	San Francisco
Cordell, Mark N.	212038	San Francisco
Cordell, Natasha LaNa	215678	San Francisco
Darnes, Ollie II	213017	San Francisco
Darnes, Searcy	213017	San Francisco
Douglas, Joyce	212150	San Francisco
Duckett, Ronald	213020	San Francisco
Harrell, Joanette B.	212675	San Francisco
Lawrence, Jameel	207312	San Francisco
Lawrence, Nawab	208849	San Francisco
Smith, Kelin K.	122674	San Francisco
Stone, Tracy	213018	San Francisco
Touchette, Michelle E.	213012	San Francsico

Tim Stoen, who helped draft the guardianship papers in the early years, stated that not only did Jones want to break up the family unit quickly, he also wanted the children to "grow up with those [of us] who were more committed and loyal to him." No one was exempt from this divide-and-conquer approach. Even such members as the Touchette and Cordell families, who loyally followed the minister from his early days in Indiana, were each forced to sign over a child in guardianship to other members of the Temple. In turn, Jones made both Joyce Touchette and Barbara Cordell guardians of other children.

J. R. Purifoy, a contractor and member of People's Temple for four years, recalled how Jones tried for several years to get him and his wife to sign guardianship papers on their children, but they stood firm. Later, however, and without any legal sanction, Jones resolutely had the children removed from their home anyway, admitting to Purifoy that this was a way of keeping people faithful to the cause: "If they [the parents] want to keep their children safe, they won't create any problems for us."

From the start, Jones concentrated on securing foster care children, and this strategy paid off. The church began to realize increasing profits from the monthly allocations received by foster care parents who, responding to their charismatic leader's public praise of them, handed over more and more money for church offerings and spent less and less on their wards. Later, when communal living quarters were set up for the children, the child-allowance checks were simply turned over to the Temple in toto.

Mendocino County welfare director Dennis Denny estimated that Jones had as many as 150 foster care children over a period of seven or eight years.

We finally told the Temple: "Either get the foster homes licensed or get them out of Mendocino County." They circumvented that by securing guardianships on some of the children. When you are a parent or a guardian, you don't have to be licensed in California to care for children. Consequently, there would be no supervision . . . no one investigating a damned thing except the guardianship in the court.

Another file found in the San Francisco People's Temple revealed that its lawyers had closely studied every conceivable statute dealing with marriage, divorce, foster care, adoption, dependent and neglected children, juvenile delinquency, and court guardianships in the state. They wanted to be certain that there would be little cause for scrutiny or supervision from officials who would be making life-affecting decisions on the children. Face-to-face contact with authorities encouraged more questions, and for that reason, special priority was given to avoiding court appearances for guardianships—as witnessed in the following note from lawyer Eugene Chaikin to his secretary, June Crym, and Tim Stoen on November 21, 1975:

Los Angeles

The judge determines if appearance is required; if papers are stamped JTD, then appearance would be necessary. But, can call two days before hearing and the clerk will tell if the recommendation is for approval—in which case no appearance would be required.

Contra Costa

Appearance is usually not necessary, if all the particulars are given and are in order. Request on the transmittal letter the date of hearing. Ten days' notice is required. After date is set, send up the order for termination and state that attorney does not intend to appear unless requested by

Court. If no request to appear is sent, then would not have to be there, but should check with probate clerk to be sure.

Alameda

Would have to ask Alameda County Counsel, Chuck Harrington, 874-7272; sometimes "he's a nice guy" according to the public defender's office.

Here is another example of evading a courtroom appearance.

I, Denise Holmes, declare:

I am the mother of Ramona LaMothe, who was born on the 29th day of July, 1970.
At the time of her birth, I was not married. Her father is Kenneth LaMothe.
I am not well, physically or mentally, sufficiently to care for this child. I wish the child to be cared for by Cleave and Paulette Jackson of 1119 Dora Street, Ukiah, California, who have agreed to do so. I ask the court to appoint Cleave and Paulette Jackson the guardians of the child. I hereby waive notice of the hearing on the petition for guardianship.
I declare under penalty of perjury that the foregoing is true and correct.
Dated at Camarillo, California, on June 21, 1973.

This signed and witnessed waiver at least gave the appearance of legality, but others bore only the mother's signature and were simply blank, signed papers for the mass production of guardianships. Jeannie Mills reported, "It was common for parents to be asked to sign a battery of forms—from confessions of abuse and neglect, of abnormal sex acts and subversion and sabotage, to legal documents giving up all claims to real estate, bank accounts, savings, inheritances, and even their own children."

The reasons for guardianships that Temple lawyers gave the judges and courts of California were both varied and creative. A close look at the files in their entirety revealed obvious lies and contradictions. Some petitions claimed medical needs; others mentioned a desire for better education, a better neighborhood, a rural setting, more family stability, and a father figure. Children living in Los Angeles needed "out of town" medical attention in San Francisco, while others living with parents in San Francisco "had to get special treatment in Los Angeles."

Following is a portion of a typical guardianship petition of People's Temple:

> Guardianship of the Person of, Estate of, RONALD CAMPBELL, a Minor, No. 213013, SUPERIOR COURT OF THE STATE OF CALIFORNIA FOR THE CITY AND COUNTY OF SAN FRANCISCO.
> .... It is necessary and convenient that a guardian or guardians be appointed for the person of said minor for the following reasons: The mother of the child wishes him to live in a structured, loving home with mother-father images, which she is unable to provide at this time and which petitioners are willing and able to provide. Petitioners and mother of the minor are friends, visit each other often, and it is mutually agreeable for the petitioners to care for said minor.

In a similar fashion, Kelin Kirtas Smith was taken from his parents, Gladys and David, three brothers, and two sisters and placed under the guardianship of Bob and Joyce Houston for a "more structured home life." (Ironically, his guardian, Bob, was rarely home. He held down two jobs and was totally involved in Temple matters—until his defection and subsequent mysterious death.) In an effort to head off any inquiries from an interested and puzzled aunt of the boy's, Gene Chaikin composed a propitiating letter for Joyce Houston to send to the woman:

... to satisfy the State legal requirements, we went to court to seek guardianship of Kirtas so the school authorities would be satisfied we are legally entitled to have him in our home. David and Gladys come visit almost every week and it's almost as if they lived with us. The enclosed notice is sent to you in accordance with court regulations. You are not required to appear at the hearing. Please be assured guardianship is nothing like an adoption; it is a temporary action to set up a legal parental situation while the child is not living with the parent.

Many children were not only taken from their parents but also separated from brothers and sisters. Little Christopher Buckley's sister, Dorothy Helen, was placed with the Janero family because "she needed a father figure," while the Mendocino County courts handed the boy over to Jones' 300-pound henchman and bodyguard, Jim McElvane: "Minor needs a father image and the educational environment which petitioner [mother] cannot offer because of long hours of work in the hospital." A few months after McElvane became Chris' legal guardian, he personally supervised the slaughter of more than thirty dogs that Jones had given shelter to in Redwood Valley—the dogs having been a successful publicity gimmick that Jones no longer felt he could afford.

In almost every instance of guardianship placement, relatives of the child expressed interest and concern for his or her sudden withdrawal from the family. Such was the case with fourteen-year-old Cornelius Lee Truss. Ignoring the fact that his immediate family consisted of both parents, two grandfathers, one grandmother, three uncles, and two aunts, the courts again nodded their approval, and Cornelius was thrown into Jim Jones' guardianship mill.

For the most part, the parents of People's Temple caused no problems. Among them was Mrs. Alta Sellers, who listened spellbound one Sunday afternoon in People's Temple, Los Angeles, as Jones dramatically meditated. She was, in her own words, "psyched out" when the minister's voice suddenly boomed: "Marvin Sellers, come to Redwood Valley for safety and work!" Within an hour Mrs. Sellers was seated in a room of the church with lawyer Gene Chaikin and a silent Jones, signing away her twelve-year-old son, Marvin, under a state guardianship.

Marvin's guardians were Richard and Clare Janero, church members and caretakers of Happy Acres, a state-licensed home for the mentally retarded in Redwood Valley, outside San Francisco. The Janeros remitted all their state receipts and other profits to Jones, who, in turn, supplied Happy Acres with free child labor.

Marvin Sellers was far from retarded himself. He was an excellent student and dreamed of becoming a doctor. His intelligence ultimately saved his mother's life. The boy was sent to Jonestown without his mother and without her knowledge, a hostage tactic that Jones used to lure parents to Guyana. But Marvin quickly discovered the truth about the jungle settlement. Two weeks before the November 18 massacre, he learned his mother intended to follow him there and he wrote her three letters, including one that was addressed to her in care of an uncle who was a retired Navy man.

Mrs. Sellers was particularly puzzled by the word "flies" written at the bottom of the letter. But it didn't puzzle the uncle, who realized the boy was using some Navy terminology he had taught him. "Flies," he told his sister-in-law, "that's a code. It's a warning. It's telling you, 'Warning! Danger! Stay where you are!'" Mrs. Sellers canceled her travel plans. Marvin Sellers was killed with cyanide in the same building where he had written the letters.

Jones knew that the whole guardianship strategy was vulnerable, and for that reason, any inquiries from interested persons were tenaciously stonewalled. Such was the case involving five-year-old Melita Nicole Gibson, whose guardianship gave People's Temple at least $2,480 annually (not including her father's support checks). On April 12, and again on June 7, 1976, Melita's father, Leroy Gibson, wrote to Chaikin from Grambling, Louisiana:

> I have received the petition of Exie Elleby for guardianship and estate of MELITA NICOLE GIBSON, a Minor. Kindly send to the above address a copy of the final petition decree stating the action of the court concerning the guardianship.

Still another letter, dated August 20, 1976, continued to request a copy of the legal guardianship:

> . . . thank you for your letter of August 13, 1976. I would appreciate very much if you could send the copy of the guardianship order on or before August 31, 1976, due to the fact that I am still sending child-support payments to my ex-wife for Melita and was unaware where the child was.

This letter prompted an interoffice memo from Chaikin's secretary:

> Jean Gibson's baby daughter, Melita, is taken care of by Exie Elleby in Los Angeles, a senior citizen, who has guardianship of the child. When we did the guardianship, we served notice on the father of the child in Louisiana, who wrote back and said he wanted a copy of the final order. We figure he wants it so he can use it to stop sending support payments. Guardianship does not absolve him of support responsibility, but he may try. Gene wanted several opinions on whether we should send him the order.

Needless to say, Leroy Gibson never received the final decree.

Defections of adults from People's Temple were given swift and decisive action. The errant members were harassed, discredited, threatened, and, in some cases, physically harmed. Even suspicious deaths were reported. But the major thrust in dealing with restive members was to make certain that their children remained under direct jurisdiction of Jim Jones, regardless of whether they were natural children or under guardianship.

Al and Deanna Mertle (alias Al and Jeannie Mills) were faithful, dedicated participants: Al was the church's photographer and Deanna was publications director. They were loving and caring people whose home became a shelter of warmth and security for many young people, especially children who were attached to the Temple. Among the latter were Patricia and Paul Anthony Petitt, whom the Superior Court of California placed under guardianship of Deanna, and Searcy, Ollie, and Najah Darnes.

After the Mertles left the church, Jones had Anita Petitt, Patricia and Paul's mother, petition the court to remove Deanna as legal guardian of her children for the following reason:

> . . . said guardian has failed, neglected, and refused, and continues to fail, neglect, and refuse, to provide for the needs of said minors, maintain or obtain appropriate living conditions for said minors, obtain medical treatment for said wards, or in any manner perform her duties as the guardian of said wards.

The petition, filed by Chaikin, asked the court to appoint Juanita Harris and Carolyn Looman as the legal guardians because there was still "continuing need for guardianship."

On February 18, 1976, a notice of the hearing on Court

Order No. 207576, for the "removal of guardian for cause," was said to have been mailed to Deanna, but Mrs. Mertle never received it and was unaware of the matter until April 13, 1976, when two hand-picked guardians took over the children. For the next two years, until the disaster in Guyana, Patricia and Paul Anthony Petitt lived in the San Francisco church of People's Temple, where, according to interviews with them, they were never taught simple numbers or colors and could not read. They were constantly threatened with the dreaded "blue-eyed monster" if they acted up or got into trouble. But they survived.

Searcy, Ollie, and Najah Darnes were not so lucky. After the Mertles were forced to leave them at the Temple, they were placed under the guardianship of Ronald James. When little Searcy saw Deanna leaving the church for the last time, he pleaded, "We don't like it here, Mommy. Please let us move back with you!" Less than a year later, the boy was raped by a thirty-year-old man, then forced to watch as a guard beat the man's penis till it bled. Searcy, Ollie, and Najah, who never knew their real father—he died when they were still infants—went to Guyana and perished.

One of the most enlightening files deals with Michele Margaret Brady and her sister, Georgiann. The Bradys' natural father, George Brady, a serviceman stationed at Fort Belvoir, Virginia, had lost track of the children for several years. He believed they were with their mother, whom he had been unable to contact. He had no information about or understanding of why the children had been placed in a guardianship situation. Nor did he know his wife or children were in Guyana until his brother informed him of their death.

The Brady guardianship brought panic to People's

Temple when its lawyers forgot to account, fraudulently, for the $2,844 they had misused from the government-supported estates of the two children. According to William S. Johnstone, Jr., a Pasadena, California, lawyer an expert on guardian- and conservatorships, "The only way in which guardians are accountable is a mandatory annual financial statement of expenses to the court, but no expenditure receipts are necessary."

In late December 1977, June Crym opened Chaikin's mail to find a court order from Judge Authur B. Broaddus:

> In the matter of the guardianship of the Persons and Estate of Michele Brady, Georgiann Brady, minors . . . this guardianship having come on for review because no annual account has been filed, the court notes that there was a purported substitution of attorneys which has not been and is not approved by the court. The attorney for the guardianship is ordered to prepare and file an accounting forthwith. Pending approval of the accounting, all powers of the guardians of the minors are suspended and the attorney, Eugene Chaikin, is directed to notify parties paying funds to the guardians or holding guardianship funds.

Crym immediately typed the following long, but important, memo to the high officials of People's Temple:

> Attached is an order issued by Judge Broaddus this week against the guardianship of Michele and Georgiann Brady; received today in mail.
>
> Maureen Fitch and Debbie Schroeder are guardians of the persons and estate of Michele and Georgiann. The estate of the children is social security they receive because their parents are dead.
>
> Every year we have had to file an "annual accounting" with the Ukiah court explaining how the guardians spent the money of the children: the social security benefits, and afdc if any was received.

Before Chaikin left, we talked a lot about what to do with guardianships that have estates that require yearly accountings and the children are overseas. We ended up hoping that if we filed substitutions of attorneys getting Chaikin off the record as attorney and placing the guardians in as attorneys for themselves, whatever happened would not come back to Chaikin. However, we were never sure what would happen when we reached the stage of an accounting being due and how the court would react.

In this case, I filed the substitution of attorneys to get Chaikin off record but never got an endorsed copy back from the court; later I noticed that I had forgotten to type in Maureen's address under her name, which is required on substitutions of attorneys so that once the attorney is removed from the court record, the court has an address for the guardian. This may be the reason that the court decided not to approve the substitution of attorneys, as it states in the attached order. The hearing for the accounting was scheduled by the Ukiah court for Dec. 9; we received notice last week, too late, so I called the judge's office and continued it to Jan. 6. The judge's secretary confirmed that it was continued to Jan. 6 so I assumed there was nothing more required until we filed the accounting. But apparently, the judge heard the case anyway and saw that the accounting was not filed, and issued this order.

However, the most important thing about this order is that

1. all powers of the guardians of the minors are suspended pending approval of the accounting (this means they are not considered guardians at this time until an accounting is approved by the court);
2. the attorney, Chaikin, is directed to notify parties paying funds to the guardians (social security administration) of this suspension;
3. the accounting must be filed with Chaikin as attorney of record, and with this minute order, I'm sure they will require a court appearance and direct the attorney to explain why an accounting has not been filed, etc. Might ask where are the guardians, children, etc.

Finally, the children and the guardians are out of state. There is no court permission in this case for the children and the guardians to be out of the state. Debbie Schroeder obviously can't return.

We better ask Garry or Pat about this and see if we can get an attorney in his firm to appear in Ukiah for the accounting, which is now set for *January 13, 1978*. Maybe Garry could do some fast talking over the phone with Judge to avoid a court appearance.

The accounting was typed up several months ago and returned from Guyana signed by Maureen, so it can be filed. The figures are just estimates, based on incomplete records as Robin's records only go back 6 months and Guyana said they had nothing. See attached. Needs Chaikin's signature.

The Temple's written strategy—to fraudulently report how the public funds were spent, and to again avoid a direct confrontation by saying that Chaikin, the mother, and the children were out of the country—worked. A few weeks later, an "Order Approving Guardians' Fourth Annual Account and Report" was endorsed and filed with the Mendocino County Clerk:

> MAUREEN FITCH and DEBBIE SCHROEDER, as guardians of the above-named wards, having heretofore filed with the Clerk of the Court their fourth annual account and report from July 1976 to August 1977, and the matter coming on regularly for hearing this day, and it appearing to the Court that due and legal notice of the hearing has been given in all respects as required by law, and no one appearing to object to or contest the account, the Court, after hearing the evidence, approves the notice given and finds the account and report to be true and correct. IT IS ORDERED that the fourth annual account and report of the guardians be, and the same is hereby, approved, allowed, and settled in all respects as set forth therein, and all acts of

the guardians as shown and set forth in the fourth annual account and report, including payment by the guardians of each and all of the items of disbursement as shown therein, are hereby specifically approved.

Following is the third annual account of the guardianship and estate of nine-year-old Michele and ten-year-old Georgiann Brady—Eugene Chaikin's monthly breakdown of expenses against the children's annual estate of $2,844 ($1,464 in Social Security benefits plus $1,380 AFDC benefits). The fourth annual account, as well as the entries for other months, is almost identical:

DISBURSEMENTS: JULY 1975

ITEM	AMOUNT
Food	$ 134.00
Allowance	20.00
Vitamins	23.00
Clothing	40.00
Entertainment	20.00
	237.00
	×12 months
	$2844.00 annual expenses

"Fraudulent" is how Grace Stoen described all the guardianship accounts:

> Most of the food was free, such as day-old doughnuts and bread, with government-surplus peanut butter, and powdered milk to wash it down. Clothing was Salvation Army and Goodwill castoffs. Any entertainment, which was seldom, was free. Twenty-three dollars a month for vitamins was inflated, and the twenty dollars listed for an allowance was simply not accurate.

However, since expenditure receipts were not required, the author was free to write his own story.

Michaeleen Brady joined her children, Michele and Georgiann, late in 1977 in Guyana, where she died with them. Her $57,000 estate disappeared into the church's bank accounts. This was not unusual: Interviews with relatives have revealed a definite pattern. Any assets a guardianship child may have had—from Julie Ann Runnels' $495 to Christine Talley's trust fund of between $30,000 and $60,000—vanished into the vast holdings of People's Temple.

Although there are varied legal opinions among California experts on just how far the state should go to protect its young wards, the nationally prominent Legal Services for Children, Inc., based in San Francisco, feels that the state and/or the courts have a legal and moral obligation to protect youngsters placed within their governmental system: First, if the guardian is a nonrelative, the Department of Health must investigate the home to determine if it is suitable. Second, the child must be assigned a social worker to ascertain if he or she is being cared for properly. There is no record that this was ever done with People's Temple guardianships. The courts simply gave total control of children to the adults of People's Temple who were not their natural parents. One social worker in San Francisco said, "Jones' political power was well known, and we knew not to hassle him or else our jobs would be on the line. Therefore, we didn't check on the children within People's Temple. It was too much of a political time bomb!" Finally, while wards may leave the state for vacations, they cannot change their residence. Yet thirty-five children were taken out of state permanently and the state did nothing, even when relatives begged for investigations and help.

Rhonda Kloempken, chairwoman of the California State Foster Care Association, stated that "if out of the tragedy we could have one reform, namely, curbing the power of judges to make direct placements . . . the death of those poor children will not be in vain."

Young Philip Lacy took the law and reform into his own hands. After spending six years under guardianship in People's Temple, first with Richard Cordell and then with Eugene Chaikin, Lacy tired of the beatings, the lack of freedom, and the threat of being sent to the jungle in Guyana. In violation of the ruling of the Superior Court of California in Mendocino County, Phil walked out of People's Temple and went to his father's apartment. "There," he said, "I loaded a gun and waited for Temple members to come and get me." They never came. Phil went on to attend college at San Luis Obispo. He was lucky. He lived.

> "They were my family, I loved them, and I knew I would never see them again if I would live through this experience. And my thirteen-year-old brother's eyes . . . the way he would look at me, like he was looking away from me and talking to my mother and it was curious. . . . Here is his big brother that he hasn't really had the chance to know, here is his big brother that he loves, and he is showing it in little ways . . . it was those eyes that woke me up for a long time after Jonestown. And it's those eyes that keep me from going to sleep at night . . . I was thinking that he was thirteen years old and he hadn't really had a chance to live his own life or to see what life's all about, and I thought about the other children that were there . . . and how Jones manipulated the children to get the parents to stay."
>
> Jim Cobb, ex-Temple member

3. Jim Jones Versus the Family

As members of the human species, we acquire both our biological genes and our identity from our parents, grandparents, great-grandparents, and more distant ancestors who braved the elements of life and extended the wellspring to us, the future generations. The strength of family ties cannot be denied. We have only to observe the crowded airports, train stations, bus terminals, and highways at holiday times for affirmation that the family is a fundamental essence of life. A solid family produces stable individuals with strong ideals and loyalties based on a love that springs from the depths of creation. It is the bond of a nation. At the same time, the family structure is not immune to influences that can often shake it to its core. Its real strengths make it vulnerable in times of duress for the entire unit or for individual members. It is this vulnerability upon which Jim Jones preyed.

The families of People's Temple were, for the most part, composed of innocent people who entered the church out of a sincere need to relate to their fellow human beings and to believe in something that would give their lives a greater sense of purpose. Jones lured them through a mixture of old-time religious fervor and a pure socialistic cause. The neophytes soon found themselves trapped in the well-devised plan of a madman.

The brilliant but evil use of children as hostages paved the way for Jones to amass millions of dollars, immeasurable political influence, and total power to exploit, terrorize, and control the rest of his followers. But he knew that before he could use the children effectively, he had to destroy the family unit.

In Jones' private quarters of the San Francisco Temple was a book on deprogramming young cult members: *Let Our Children Go!* by Ted Patrick. The following passage was darkly underscored, and it epitomizes the plight of the children in People's Temple:

> Once they get a victim, they consciously and deliberately set about to destroy every normal pattern of living the victim has known; he is separated from his friends, he is turned against his family . . . he is literally robbed of whatever financial assets he may possess, and his parents are, as a matter of course, blackmailed into contributing large sums of money to the cult merely in order to be occasionally permitted to see their child.

Jones did not precipitately turn families against themselves. Instead, he implemented a deliberate strategy, subtly and effectively, to achieve his desired end. Temple members found themselves kept increasingly busy, with fewer opportunities for relaxation and sleep, and this condition eventually produced a state of mental confusion. They were totally unaware that they were being brainwashed by Jones' adaptation of "the book" on mind control. Soon they were being fed a steady diet of antifamily doctrine.

Al and Jeannie Mills have related how, after some very intense and long, exhaustive hours of work, they looked forward to spending Thanksgiving with Al's parents. They sent a note to the Temple's "planning commission" requesting permission for the visit, and Jones responded:

> It's time for you to cut your family ties. This church is your family now. Blood ties are dangerous because they prevent people from being totally dedicated to the Cause.

The Millses obeyed. Shortly thereafter, they were further instructed on the rules of family relationships by Jack Beam and Linda Sharon Amos, top officials of the Temple. Jack Beam said:

> Families are a part of the enemy system. They do not love you. If you were in trouble, only Jim and his church family would be there to help you. Your family would turn their backs on you if you needed something that might cause them inconvenience. They don't understand this Cause, and therefore you cannot trust them.

Linda Amos, who later, on Jones' command, slit the throats of her three children, then her own, said:

> When you have to see your families, you are to go for just one purpose. You should make up some sad story to get them to give you money or valuables. Ask them for presents or clothes or anything you think you can get.

Another defector, Yolanda Crawford, who was in Guyana for several months in 1977, wrote in an affidavit:

Jones ordered all of us to break our ties with our families. He said that our highest and only loyalty should be the Cause, and the only reason for staying in touch with our families at all was to keep them pacified and to collect inheritances when they died off.

Families that joined the church as a unit were quickly separated through manipulation and/or slick legal work and court action—not to mention the pretense that the "socialistic body" or "cause" was much more important than the smaller unit, the family. The Purifoys, for instance, who had been steadfast in remaining a family, were promoted to the planning commission. The day their children were taken away followed twenty-four hours of intensive brainwashing by Jones' rhetoric and no sleep:

> My wife and I were at an all-night meeting and came home around 9 A.M. We met our children coming out of the house. I don't think they even knew at the time what was happening. But when my wife and I got in the house, there was someone coming out with the children's clothes. We asked where they were going. And this person said, "Father thinks it's best that the children move into someone else's house."

From then on, the Purifoys were allowed to see their children only one hour every two weeks.

Once Jones had physically separated the family members from one another, he and his top staff systematically destroyed the family fibers with an assortment of pernicious techniques and callous policies. At first he encouraged the children to call their parents by their first names—then he demanded it. Only Jones and his wife, Marceline, could be called Father and Mother. Any parent who was not supportive of People's Temple (Jim Cobb's father, for instance) was threatened and forced to leave his own home. Children and parents both were publicly rewarded for spying on each other and reporting to Jones any critical thoughts or comments expressed against him. Jones would, in turn, inform the parents or children what the other had told him, thus driving them farther apart.

Family members were forbidden to sit together at Temple services. Peer pressure was cultivated and used to break down the "chicks"—children with close family ties. One child who was in the cult for more than six years stated:

> We couldn't have a family together; we had to have other people's families. I called other people Mom and Dad because I didn't have my mom and dad with me. You know, it wasn't a normal childhood!

A Ukiah woman refused to join the Temple when her husband did. "Jones wanted my mind, and I wouldn't give it," she recalled. "He wanted my kids for someone else to raise, and I wouldn't give them up. He said we should be willing to die for him, and I'm not dying for anyone." Jones forbade her husband to have sex with her and gave him another partner. The marriage disintegrated.

Without their children and with Jones providing communal living for more and more members, the adults slowly became thoroughly convinced that their economic base—their homes—was no longer needed. Daily they were told that Jim Jones was their sole supplier of spiritual and worldly goods. Once the foundation for that rationale had been laid, the homes gradually folded, families ceased to function, and everything of value—life savings, houses, cars, furniture, jewelry, furs—was turned over to the Cause. He even had people turn in their engagement and wedding rings.* Within a few

---

* According to Grace Stoen, Jones intended to use the gold from the latter to bribe foreign governments in case they moved abroad.

years, J. R. Purifoy, a building contractor and property developer, turned over forty-four pieces of property with a net worth of over two million dollars. The records of the transfer of property deeds from May 6, 1968, to September 16, 1976, in Mendocino County alone show that approximately twenty-three members turned over thirty-three private homes and other personal properties to People's Temple at the request of Reverend J. W. Jones.

Early in his ministerial career, Jones subjected his own family to indignities and threats that ultimately would be shared by all the people he attracted. In Indiana, his wife learned of her husband's sexual indiscretions and threatened to leave him. He countered by saying he had sex with these people for "religious reasons," but that it "disgusted" him. If she ever left, he threatened, he would kill their four children. His own children were his first hostages, and the same fear tactics that succeeded with his wife would be used many more times before threat became reality.

As Jones' sexual appetite grew, whatever religious pretext existed before was now replaced with perverted acts of degradation toward a membership whose economic base was all but destroyed and whose dependency on its leader was guaranteed. He proclaimed himself absolute ruler over all matters of marriage, divorce, and childbearing. Recognizing the vital role of love and sex in stable family relationships, he banned sex, bragging that he was the only one who could really satisfy man or woman. At this point, he could even count on his wife's blessing on his so-called generosity and sacrifices.

In *Six Years with God* Jeannie Mills, formerly Deanna Mertle, recorded Marceline Jones' public statement of her approval of their arrangement:

> It's true that I have had to share my husband in the past, for the Cause. It was always painful for me because I love him

> very much, and just like everyone else, it's painful for me to see the person I love with someone else. Several years ago, Jim asked me for a divorce because I just couldn't make the adjustment to being married to a man who was also married to a Cause. At that time I had to do some serious introspection and decide on my priorities.
>
> I knew I didn't want to lose Jim, so I agreed that I would share him with people who needed to relate to the Cause on a more personal level. This has been a very difficult thing for me to live with, and it's caused me a lot of heartache. However, tonight, as I heard him pour out his heart to you, explaining the suffering he goes through when he has to use his body to serve the Cause, I realized that I have been very selfish.
>
> I want to make a public statement tonight that I am willing to share my husband for the Cause, and that I won't resent it any longer.

Mills described Jones' reaction to his wife's speech as "stunned." He then added: "I hope Marcie's unexpected offer doesn't cause a lot of you to begin making demands upon me. I am already overworked in this area." But the die was cast. From then on, an array of sexual happenings became part of the daily routine at People's Temple, both in California and in Jonestown. He appointed Patty Cartmell to make all appointments for sexual encounters with members who "need to learn to relate to the Cause." Many of these were made, however, at Jones' behest, not that of his followers.

In his lust for unlimited power over the lives of others, Jones forced men and women to lie with him and each other in adulterous and homosexual depravities, in private and in public. On one occasion, a husband whose wife complained that he had never had oral sex with her was ordered by Jones to do so with a woman who was menstruating, while 125 people, including his wife, were forced to watch. Although such instances must surely have destroyed the dignity and self-esteem of participants and observers alike, according to Tim Carter, a survivor of Jonestown, "Dad knows best" or "Just do as Dad tells you" was the attitude that prevailed, enabling Jones to dominate everyone's sexual life. "He told the husbands he only did it to help the women, but he also did it to emasculate the men of Jonestown."

The children, in their formative years, watched and listened and learned as these loathsome experiences unfolded before their young eyes. They observed someone's father being humiliated by another man; someone else's mother engaging in sex with another woman; and stood with the entire population of Jonestown and saw one of their playmates being forced to masturbate herself because her parents had been discovered having a private conversation.

The children listened. When Jones wasn't engaged in sex, he was talking about it, always in their presence. They had no choice but to listen as Jones boasted of his sexual prowess. The five-year-olds were forced to learn the following chant: "We cut off the penises of capitalists and people who believe in God." The devastating effect of all this on the ego of a developing child or a sensitive teen-ager could only be immense, and on the family it was total. That was the master plan of Jim Jones.

In her affidavit of April 10, 1978, Yolanda Crawford said, "I recall several instances of Jim Jones stating he could silence critics or defectors by accusing them of being homosexuals, child abusers, terrorists, or sexual deviates." While this is likely, it wasn't even necessary for Jones to accuse anyone. Early on he had all his followers confess, on paper, that they engaged in perverted sexual and other unacceptable forms of behavior.

These signed confessions were used to keep everyone in line or, in the case of defection, to discredit anything the individual might have revealed.

Such was the case in the custody battle between Jim Jones and Grace and Tim Stoen. During the court battle that ensued after John Victor Stoen had been whisked off to Guyana instead of being returned to his parents, Jones, through his aides, released the following incriminating document:

> I, Timothy Oliver Stoen, hereby acknowledge that in April, 1971, I entreated my beloved pastor, James W. Jones, to sire a child by my wife, Grace Lucy (Grech) Stoen, who had previously, at my insistence, reluctantly but graciously consented thereto. James W. Jones agreed to do so, reluctantly, but I explained that I very much wished to raise a child, but was unable, after extensive attempts, to sire one myself. My reason for requesting James W. Jones to do this is that I wanted my child to be fathered, if not by me, by the most compassionate, honest and courageous human being the world contains.
>
> The child, John Victor Stoen, was born on January 25, 1972. I am privileged beyond words to have the responsibility for caring for him, and I undertake this task humbly with the steadfast hope that said child will become a devoted follower of Jesus Christ and be instrumental in bringing God's kingdom here on earth, as has been his wonderful natural father.

With such documents, Jones was certain that he could destroy, or at least neutralize, the credibility of all his would-be defectors and critics. In most cases, he succeeded.

By early 1977, a few people within the media had accumulated enough strange, though unconfirmed, stories about People's Temple and the abuse of children, families, and the legal system to warrant further investigation. Word got out that the publication *New West* was working on an exposé of the Temple and its well-known minister, Jim Jones.

While Jones tried desperately to kill the *New West* story, using his powerful political allies that ranged from the John Birch Society to the American Civil Liberties Union, he was not without additional recourse. For many months, unknown to anyone except those in the trusted inner circle, he had been making elaborate plans to flee the United States for the jungle settlement in Guyana.

Parents were told to sign forms (already notarized) that allowed:

- Power of Attorney: "I give each of the attorneys-in-fact the right to care, custody, supervision, and control of said minor anywhere throughout the world, and to travel anywhere with said minor throughout the world."
- State of Custody: "Complete and exclusive obligation for the care and control" of children during travel and stay.
- Assets (including cash) to be imputed to the People's Temple Agriculture Mission.
- Waiver of any obligation to pay for any transportation home.
- Release from responsibility on the part of People's Temple for any property that children or parents "may leave behind."
- Loyalty Pledge to Jim Jones: ". . . Pastor Jim Jones has the highest character I have ever known. I fully believe in his honesty and integrity and thank him for all he has done for me."

The code word assigned to the operation was "HOUSTON." Here again, the children were to play the key role of hostages. Just as they had been used to keep their parents in the Temple's active membership in California, they would now be used to force their parents to follow them to a foreign land.

By the early summer of 1977, Operation Houston was in high gear. The majority of the children were quickly and quietly uprooted. With all the necessary forms signed in advance by unknowing parents, the youngsters were packed on a bus, shipped across the United States to either New York or Miami, and then flown out of the country. Patricia Lee Grunnet, legal guardian of Nawab Lawrence, took him and twenty-five other children in the first load. (Grunnet was a completely loyal staff person and was therefore entrusted with the initial shipment of children without their parents.) Two hundred and fifty other young people followed as Jones and his lawyers instructed the staff that passport applications were to be stamped "Reason for Leaving Country: Vacation." As young Bernadette Jackson reflected, "The reason for leaving is vacation . . . vacation . . . a long, long, long vacation." On the immigration applications to Guyana itself, however, the reason given for entering the country (filled out by the People's Temple staff) was "Permanent Residence."

When the travelers landed at Georgetown, they were quickly processed, then packed into a shrimp boat owned by People's Temple for a twenty-six-hour trip to the jungle settlement. The boat was approved to carry eight adults safely; Operation Houston would see as many as eighty people packed together on a modern-day slave boat, headed for real bondage in Jonestown. Once there, Jones ordered all forms of identification turned over to his lieutenants. Confiscated items included passports, drivers' licenses, credit cards, Social Security cards, checkbooks, savings accounts, cash, and even wristwatches.

Within a period of three months, Operation Houston was complete: All the children of People's Temple had left the United States to rendezvous with hunger, humiliation, terror, and death in a country of which they knew nothing.

So sudden was the exodus of children that most relatives were taken completely by surprise. When Beverly and Howard Oliver, who were not Temple members, left for work that morning, their teen-age sons, Bruce and William, were asleep in their beds. By the time the parents came home, their sons were on their way to Guyana. Grace and Tim Stoen discovered weeks later that their little boy, John, had been ordered to Jonestown in the company of nineteen-year-old Maria Katsaris, whose own father, Steven, didn't know she had left the United States until he received a letter from her. Jim Cobb and Mickey Touchette found out by chance, months later, that their respective brothers and sisters were out of the country. The same thing happened to Don Ponts and Lawrence Tupper and their children. And Robert and Nadyne Houston thought their grandchildren were going to New York City on vacation.

Jim Cobb was one of the first to act. Responding to Jones' implied threat of "revolutionary suicide" on June 22, 1978, he filed a suit for compensatory and punitive damages for "intentional infliction" of emotional distress against James Warren Jones and the People's Temple in the Superior Court of California in San Francisco.

> Plaintiff is informed and believes and thereon alleges that defendant then and there referred to such a threat euphemistically as a threat of "revolutionary suicide" when, in actuality, it was a megalomaniacal threat of "mass murder," which would result in the death of minor children not old enough to make a voluntary and informed decision about serious matters of any nature, much less insane proposals of collective suicide.

The *New West* article, "Inside People's Temple"—in retrospect what seems to be a very mild questioning of some of the more lurid goings-on at People's Temple—by Marshall Kilduff and Phil Tracy, had appeared on August 1, 1977, but Jonestown was already established and settled. The story had an important side effect, however: Former Temple members who were living isolated in fear began to talk with one another and share common experiences and deep concerns about their relatives who were still involved with Jim Jones.

Phone conversations turned into meetings, and because of those meetings, people who had once feared Jones and his armed bodyguards were now ready to fight. Out of a basic family love and longing for imprisoned daughters, sons, parents, and grandchildren, the organization of Concerned Relatives came into being to challenge Jones, with the aim of rebuilding the families Jones had destroyed and returning its loved ones to society as functioning, free-thinking human beings.

The Concerned Relatives hired lawyers and began to wage an unrelenting, grass-roots-style campaign against Jones. They gathered signatures for petitions and sent letters and affidavits to Congress and to state and federal agencies; they badgered the media; they picketed and demonstrated, presenting their case to local and national religious officials and anyone else who would listen.

Starting in September 1977, five of the Concerned Relatives made trips to Guyana in attempts to see their children, with little or no success. Steven Katsaris made two separate trips to see his daughter, Maria. The first time, he brought with him a letter from her asking him to come, but the U.S. Embassy in Guyana told him that she refused to see him, claiming "he had molested her." Returning to Guyana a month and a half later, he was allowed to see her briefly, but only in the presence of three other Temple members.

In January 1978, Tim and Grace Stoen arrived in Guyana armed with a California court order for custody of their son, John Victor, but this meant nothing to Jones, who refused to let either parent see the child and threatened their lives if they did not drop legal proceedings against him.

Nevertheless, Jones was feeling the heat. On March 14, 1978, he sent a letter, written on Temple stationery, to every member of Congress, complaining of "bureaucratic harassment." The letter ended with the following:

> [I]t is equally evident that people cannot forever be continually harassed and beleaguered by such tactics without seeking alternatives that have been presented. I can say without hesitation that we are devoted to a decision that it is better even to die than to be constantly harassed from one continent to the next.

Though such a threat might have been dismissed as hyperbole by most people, the Concerned Relatives knew better. On April 11, they issued a detailed open letter to Jones, which they delivered to every important official in California and Washington. In this "Accusation of Human Rights Violations by Rev. James Warren Jones Against Our Children and Relatives at the People's Temple Jungle Encampment in Guyana, South America" which is printed in its entirety in the Appendix, the parents charged Jones with violations of the United Nations Charter, the Universal Declaration of Human Rights, the U.S. Constitution, and the Constitution of Guyana, for the following:

1. Making the following threat calculated to cause alarm for the lives of our relatives: "I can say without hesitation that we are devoted to a decision that it is better even to die than to be constantly harassed from one continent to the next."
2. Employing physical intimidation and psychological

coercion as part of a mind-programming campaign aimed at destroying family ties, discrediting belief in God, and causing contempt for the United States of America.
3. Prohibiting our relatives from leaving Guyana by confiscating their passports and money and by stationing guards around Jonestown to prevent anyone escaping.
4. Depriving them of their right to privacy, free speech, and freedom of association by:
   a. Prohibiting telephone calls;
   b. Prohibiting individual contacts with "outsiders";
   c. Censoring all incoming and outgoing mail;
   d. Extorting silence from relatives in the U.S. by threats to stop all communication;
   e. Preventing our children from seeing us when we travel to Guyana.

After spelling out these charges in detail, the relatives concluded with the demands that Jones:

1. Publicly answer our questions regarding your threat of a collective "decision . . . to die," and publicly promise U.S. Secretary of State Cyrus Vance and Guyana Prime Minister Forbes Burnham that you will never encourage or solicit the death of any person at Jonestown, whether individually or collectively, for any reason whatsoever;
2. Remove all guards physically preventing our relatives from leaving Jonestown;
3. Return all passports and money taken from our relatives to them for their permanent possession;
4. Permit and encourage our relatives a one-week visit home, at our expense. (Because our relatives have been in Guyana for months—and some for years—and because it is our belief that they do not know the full People's Temple story and have been prejudiced against their families, we demand you demonstrate in practice your contention that they are their own agents

by permitting and encouraging our relatives to visit their families in the United States for one week, with our guarantee that we will provide them with round trip air fare and not interfere with their return at the end of the family visit should they so choose.)
5. Permit our relatives to write letters to whomever they wish, uncensored and in private.
6. Permit our relatives to read letters sent to them in private and without censorship.
7. Abide by the orders of the courts in the United States which you have heretofore ignored.
8. Notify us within three days on your radio-phone network of your full acceptance and compliance with these demands by contacting: Steven A. Katsaris, Trinity School, 915 West Church Street, Ukiah, California 95482, telephone (707) 462-8721.

Jones and company struck back in a press release dated May 10, 1978:

The statement of the "Concerned Relatives" was signed by a sordid crew of individuals who, among other things, have tried to blackmail; have embezzled from People's Temple while infiltrating it; have even been involved in the manufacture of ammunition and have advocated ridiculous and mad schemes of violence in order to achieve revolutionary "ends" in the classic manner of agent-provocateurs. Included in the group are people who have used and trafficked in drugs; some have molested children, including their own . . . have operated credit card rackets, forged checks, stolen money from the treasury in the amount of thousands of dollars, and have actually abused and treated black youngsters as house slaves . . .

They have circulated lies about us everywhere and have even tried to send undercover agents hired to snatch away children illegally and violently from their rightful parents and homes . . . With the help of their lawyer, Tim Stoen, the group has put together a document that is filled with distortions, misportrayals, and lies . . .

Attached to the press release was a note on one of the leaders of the Concerned Relatives that alleged he "forced young men and women to bow before him and kiss his genitals, calling them racist pigs if they refused to do so."

To the very end, the Concerned Relatives wouldn't give up. At their own expense, fourteen members accompanied Congressman Leo Ryan to Guyana and sought help at the U.S. Embassy in Georgetown. To their bitter disappointment, the Embassy staff showed them a slide presentation of Jonestown and the smiling children whom they knew and wanted to see freed. Grace Stoen told how the group collectively broke down in tears as the impact of the Ambassador's words, "We can't help you," hit them. "Beaten and broken," in the words of Stoen, they could only hope the Ryan party would be successful in Jonestown.

One year before, Mickey Touchette, one of the first seven Temple members to defect in 1973, had been briefly united with her relatives in Guyana by an international phone call. Because Jones was monitoring the call and the Touchette family knew it, much of their conversation consisted of party-line slurs and charges against Mickey. But she knew the game, knew the line, and would have none of it. The dialogue between granddaughter and grandfather captured the feelings of people separated, of family roots, and of anguish.

> MICKEY: Grandpa, I want you to know that I've got your first great-grandchild here. Would you like to see him when you get back to the United States?
>
> GRANDFATHER: This is the most beautiful place in the world. Goodbye.
>
> MICKEY: I hear that, Grandpa. All of you are telling me what a beautiful place that jungle is. That's fine. What I'm telling you is that when you decide to leave there, I'm

here in San Francisco. I'm here waiting on you. I want to have another Christmas, I want to have another Thanksgiving, I want to have a family. I want you all to get out of there as soon as you can. . . .

With the exception of Mickey's father and brother, the Touchette family perished, as did the Oliver boys, the Houston girls, Dona Ponts, and the Tupper children.

Jim Cobb joined People's Temple in 1967, along with his entire family except for his father. He defected in 1973, while he was attending college. The first major defection, he took six others with him, including Mickey Touchette. Cobb was a thorn in Jones' organizational side from then on. When word came that Cobb was accompanying Congressman Ryan's fact-finding group to Jonestown, Jones ordered him killed at the airstrip, as well as the Representative from California and his investigating party. As long as Cobb lived, he was a threat to Jones' struggle for omnipotence. He represented the audacity to think critically and to fight for family roots. Worst of all, if he successfully convinced the rest of his family to leave Guyana, Jones knew this could start a mass defection and bring about the downfall of his financial empire.

Jim Cobb went to Guyana with a strong premonition that he would die, but he wanted to save his mother, three sisters, and two brothers, and he was prepared for the worst. When the firing began at the airstrip, Jim escaped into the jungle. His family was not so fortunate. All of them lost their lives but his brother Johnny, who was in Georgetown that day. The following day Johnny returned to Jonestown to find identification tags on their dead mother, Eloise Christine, aged fifty; three sisters, Sharon, Sandra, and Brenda; and thirteen-year-old brother, Joel.

In a joint interview with *NBC News* and the *Chicago Sun-Times,* Jim Cobb reflected on his family:

> It started to rain as I started to leave Jonestown, and just before it rained Don Harris was trying to find us for an interview, a family interview. And at the time, I didn't feel up to it at all. I felt like just being with them, and I didn't have much to say.
>
> But after the interview, it rained, and my mother and myself talked for a short while underneath one of the awnings on the little house, the little cottage, and I told her that I loved her, and I told her that I loved the rest of the family more than I could express to her. And she said, "I love you, too." And at that time I asked her, "Would you please come home? Some other time, not now? To visit me?" And she said, "Yes."
>
> And my younger brother had on some shoes that were dress shoes, sort of—they weren't for walking in the mud—and I told him that I'd take my bag here so that he wouldn't have to walk through the mud, and he said, "That's OK." And as we were walking, my body just started doing things that I didn't even recognize.
>
> My heart was really thumping hard, and the voices said, "Come back!" And as I was walking to the truck, a thought flashed in my head, and I wished that I could take him by the hand and we could disappear. And I took the bag from him, and I said, "I love you, Joel, and I'll see you later." And he told me, "Bye." And he whispered, "I love you."
>
> He turned away and walked back through the mud, and I looked back at him and my sister Sandy. They were looking at me and they showed a lot more than tension in their eyes, in their smiles. It was love, and I knew I would never see them again.

> *"I had a little boy in my room and his name was Stanley Gigg, and he was roly-poly and he had awful trouble learning to read and to write, but I liked him very much. The only thing in the whole world that Stanley wanted to do was be a carpenter. He was building a house down by the creek while in fourth grade, yet he was the one who drove the tractor in Guyana that brought the men out who gunned down Ryan. I just don't see how anybody could change that little boy who wanted to be a carpenter into that kind of a murderer."*
>
> Ruby Bogner, fourth-grade teacher, Redwood, California

4. Brainwashing Dreams

Those who came under the spell of this man were made to order for his cult gospel. "Racial equality" and "social justice" were music to their ears. His preaching touched hearts, awakened dreams for an end to oppression, and offered a simple life in which, since he alone knew best, he would make the decisions for them and create a new social order.

His followers showered him with their savings, cars, jewelry, and even homes. They abandoned or gave up their children to follow a man who many believed was actually God. Some outsiders called him a crook and a racketeer, while their adult children thought him to be their very own messiah. A fleet of buses and churches in various cities funneled into his mysterious ministry the revenue that allowed it to grow from modest beginings to a multimillion-dollar operation. He fed his followers and others who were hungry. He reached out for prostitutes and drug addicts and seemed to cure his believers of cancer, heart ailments, and broken limbs and lives.

His people believed in him with such loyalty that they helped forge the movement into a powerful political army. Hard workers they were, one and all, and the mandatory communal living quarters never closed down for sleep. Political leaders flocked to his church, and he could claim to have elected a congressman, a big-city mayor, and a President.

Critics, who feared that their sons and daughters or wives, parents, or grandparents had become brainwashed slaves to this charismatic leader, took their concerns to the press. A scathing exposé opened the door to his secret world, a world filled with absolute devotion, wealth, and a harem that serviced his sexual appetites. The magazine article stated that those under his control were black and white, poor and rich, college-educated and illiterate, laborers, domestics, lawyers, and doctors. Immediately, a host of influential people came to his defense, including his own team of lawyers, claiming fraud and libel.

Was this Jim Jones? No, this was Father Divine, the man whom Jim Jones emulated in his compulsive plan to control the minds of his followers, the same kind of people Father Divine had controlled, with the same dreams and the same problems, two generations before.

Several influences on the mind of Jim Jones can be cited, among them Adolf Hitler, the subject of nearly half the books found in the small library in Jones' bedroom on the third floor of the San Francisco Temple. Another was Charles Manson, of whom Jones spoke admiringly several times to his closest aides for the national press coverage Manson had received from the Tate-LaBianca murders. But by far the most significant influence was that of George Baker, alias Father Divine.

One of the books in Jones' library was *Father Divine: Holy Husband* by Sara Harris (Doubleday, 1953), checked out of the Indianapolis Public Library and never returned. It thoroughly documents the life of a man born to poor sharecroppers on a rice plantation in Georgia, who became God along the way and refined the techniques of cultism and brainwashing as he built a multimillion-dollar religious empire on the East Coast, some twenty years before the birth of Jim Jones.

Born May 13, 1931, James Warren Jones grew up in the small Indiana community of Lynn, population 1,500. His father, a disabled World War I veteran and a member of the Ku Klux Klan, abused and neglected his son. Although Jones was not ordained a minister in the Christian Church/Disciples of Christ until 1964, he played at preacher from early in childhood, his first flock being animals. As a boy, he frequently took in animals, cared for them, won their trust, then killed them and gave them elaborate funerals, with candles and all the accouterments.

Jones was already a practicing preacher with a human congregation when he heard about Father Divine in the mid-1950s. In 1957 or 1958, he visited Divine's Philadelphia Peace Mission and studied for a weekend. Stories of Divine's life-style—silk suits, chauffeured limousines, and a selection of women among Divine's communal followers—may have played a part in attracting Jones, but there is no doubt he returned to his flock in Indianapolis with some new and very dangerous ideas.

Like Father Divine's Peace Mission, what was to become Jim Jones' People's Temple was soon to have a godhead and an inner cabinet for the purpose of delegating authority and administering a complex and growing institution. Bright professionals were to be recruited to improve and expand operations—lawyers, accountants, architects, public relations personnel, press secretaries, personal photographers, and even a staff of doctors and nurses.

Both Divine and Jones fed the minds and bodies of the faithful, then induced them to relinquish all their worldly possessions and assets without question. They set up employment agencies and found work for those without jobs; entire paychecks were then turned over to the churches. In both operations, families were destroyed, people were placed in isolation, and sex was banned among married couples and lovers, limited to "god" only. Public confessions kept potential troublemakers or problems at minuscule levels.

Divine and Jones both sought membership among the oppressed. The majority of their followers were poor, uneducated, economically deprived, and lacking resources to break out of the poverty cycle. The following statement from a woman who belonged to the Peace Mission could just as easily have come from one who belonged to People's Temple:

> I was one of six kids. My father walked out and our mother had to work long hours. There was no supervision and the kids didn't go to school.

The same is true for what another woman said about her early life:

> Never had no toilet for just our family. I use to live on 137th Street off of Lenox Avenue, on the fifth floor. There was four other families living on that floor, too, and all five of us—twenty-six people sharing the same toilet. Most times you want to get in, somebody else got there first and you got to wait. Some hours, like early in the morning, you want to go

out looking for a job, there is a line out in front of the toilet. Only the pushers know how to push other folks around can get in there in the mornings. Me, I never used to get in. Used to be a public toilet on 125th Street, you got to walk down steps like to a subway. I used that all the time.

Membership also included the disenchanted idealists from well-educated, middle-class or wealthy families. This group formed a cadre of technocrats whose intellect and affluence insured the successful operation and expansion of the churches. The former group comprised the blind followers, the latter enjoyed more privileges and status, yet both were convinced by their leaders that their existences represented "true equality" and a "living harmony in race relations."

As early as 1915, Father Divine was preaching racial equality and social justice, performing faith healings, replacing "lost" teeth with "real" ones, and feeding his followers well. In 1927, one member described the food served every Sunday as "just like Christmas—chicken, ham, beef stew, corn, mashed potatoes, rice, hominy beans, tomatoes, cole slaw, spinach, mountainous bowls of ice cream, cakes as big as automobile tires but higher, piles of cheese, tea, coffee, Postum, milk, and chocolate milk."

A flier, circulated in Jones' early days in San Francisco, shows the striking similarities between the established master of deceit, Divine, and the apprentice, Jones:

PASTOR JIM JONES

PROPHET—Saves the lives of total strangers with his predictions. Scores will be present to give medical documentation of the amazing healing;

PUBLIC SCHOOL TEACHER AND GOVERNMENTAL OFFICIAL—Currently an active teacher in the California System;

> HEALER OF CANCEROUS DISEASES DOCTORS CALLED "IN-
> CURABLE";
>
> PASTOR OF THE NATION'S LARGEST YOUTH INTERNATIONAL
> RELIGIOUS MOVEMENT, WITH A 185-VOICE CHOIR, WILL BE
> HERE!!
>
> SPECIAL NOTICE: This message of God proclaims Apostolic
>   Social Justice of Equality and PROVES his message
>   by divine SIGNS and wonders.
>
> FREE BANQUET

Their large followings provided both leaders with leverage in the world of power politics. Divine supplied New York City and Philadelphia politicians with an open forum to come and meet his supporters. The elected officials and candidates knew that with an endorsement from Father, they need not worry about the precinct battle of getting out the voters for the right man. Fiorello La Guardia, three-time mayor of New York, spoke at the Peace Mission during his first campaign: "And I say, Father Divine, no matter what you want, I will support you."

Likewise, national, state, and local politicians and their wives visited Jim Jones to get the People's Temple endorsement and votes. More important, they wooed him for the reliable, gratis services of his membership, including children of all ages, who would, at Father's command, work unceasingly for months as campaign volunteers. Such political figures as Governor Jerry Brown, Lieutenant Governor Mervyn Dymally, District Attorney Joseph Freitas, Mayor George Moscone, Jane Fonda, and Tom Hayden spoke at People's Temple and received support from Jones. So important, too, was this new and powerful religious force in San Francisco to Jimmy Carter's campaign for the Presidency that Mrs. Carter dined privately with Jones in 1976.

It was the filing of child abuse complaints by outsiders and the subsequent court actions that made these cult leaders vulnerable to press scrutiny. During the 1930s a large number of Divine's members were taken to court "for neglect or complete abandonment of minor children." Eleven-year-old Robert Smith testified in New York City Children's Court: "Sure I need my ma. But I ain't got her, though. Father Divine's got her." One of the fathers told the judge: "He is one of them crazy preachers what send the wiminfolks crazy." But a sixty-three-year-old grandmother had this to say about giving up her three sons, two daughters, and seven grandchildren:

> It is an easy thing to do. I must put my mind to driving out any thought of them I formerly loved. Father [Divine] told me that is what I must do and so I did it. Once you recognize Father's divinity, you can do anything he instructs you to.

While young mothers who brought their children into Divine's Peace Mission were told to treat them impersonally and never to call them anything but "sister" or "brother," Jones ordered children to call their parents by their first names.

Judge Richard Hartshorne of the Common Pleas Court in New Jersey declared Divine "responsible for the promotion of family disorganizations," and New York City Children's Court Judge Jacob Panken called him "a destroyer of children" and "evil."

Divine and Jones lost followers in two ways—defection and death. Of the hundreds who defected, most remained silent out of fear of reprisals. Some fled important positions within their cult's hierarchy—personal and confidential secretaries, key financial planning assistants. Some were jealous lovers cast aside for younger women. However, when defectors were brave enough to talk publicly, both Divine and Jones discredited them by calling them liars and worse, while hundreds of the faithful came to the defense of their living gods.

When a member of the Peace Mission died, Father Divine callously had him or her thrown out like a sack of old clothes. The living buried the dead both literally and financially. In their god's cold, calculating mind, "true followers don't die." They, like him, would live forever.

Jones copied that expense-saving tactic, according to the following church bulletin, posted on the northern California public notice board:

> We've had no need to utilize such services of a funeral home since 1959. No one who has followed the teachings of Christ's works through Pastor Jones has died in all that time.

Robbed of their savings, their homes and families, their freedoms and dignity in life, they were further desecrated in death by the very "gods" who had lured them into modern bondage.

But death was the one area in which Jones finally overshadowed his teacher. His followers, whose very numbers accorded him a powerful political influence and favors, also won for him national and international recognition—at the least, a footnote to the history of the late twentieth century.

In order to understand the phenomenon of Jim Jones, which, as the comparison with Father Divine shows, was not unique in our history except for the way it ended, we must learn more about his followers. Who were they? Where did they come from? Why did they join the Temple? And how was it that they could, as a collective, programmed, and computerized entity, respond to, obey, and ultimately fall victim to their demented leader on that fateful day?

Of the 950 Americans listed as People's Temple members living in Guyana (913 of whom died on November 18, 1978), less than one-third were born in California, from where, Jones had them believe, they had emigrated as twentieth-century religious/political refugees. They came from thirty-nine states, the District of Columbia, and eight foreign countries. The largest representation came from California and Texas, with 295 and 111, respectively. Arkansas, Indiana, Mississippi, and Louisiana each gave origin to thirty-five or more of the Temple's members.

People's Temple was an ethnic rainbow, though the membership was largely black. Two-thirds were very young or very old. Their backgrounds spanned the affluent and the poor, the educated and the illiterate. Here is a sample:

RICHARD TROPP, 36: Well-educated. A former teacher of his at the University of Rochester wrote: "Mr. Tropp is one of the three or four most brilliant students I've ever taught. Truly exceptional."

VIRGINIA TAYLOR, 92: A life of hardship and racial discrimination. "I was born in 1886. I sang all kinds of songs and tried to cover up everything that would break a little child's heart."

FANN GURVICH, 25: From a well-to-do New Orleans family. Privately educated at the École Classique Academy, Newcomb College, Vassar, the University of California, and Golden Gate College's Law School in San Francisco. Loved poetry, Shakespeare, and translated Sanskrit.

RUTHIE ———, 33: Born to a sharecropping family in Mississippi, she ran away at the age of twelve to a dishwashing job. Seven years later, she was a Los Angeles prostitute and heroin addict, and was convicted of several crimes. Beaten by a homosexual pimp for over eleven years before joining People's Temple.

PAT GRUNNET, 37: Peace Corps teacher in Tanganyika for three years. Volunteered to work with the Migrant Ministry of Cesar Chavez and labored for prison reform and an end to the Vietnam war. Worked with emotionally disturbed children in Jonestown.

HENRY MERCER, 92: Born in Jessup, Georgia, and witnessed the results of lynchings as a child. ". . . it's an ugly thing to see. They'd cut your penis off and put it in your mouth." Became a labor organizer and a Communist during the Depression. "I believe that everyone should be equal."

RHODA JOHNSON, 16: "I was like a single ant in the whole world. I was nothing, going nowhere. I was bored and unhappy at home. Jones made me feel like I was someone. Just the sound of his voice made you feel like you had power. My parents were even caught up by him and they encouraged me to join him."

In fact, those who joined People's Temple were idealists. Not only were they looking for a better way of life, they sought a communion of equality, love, and brotherhood. They believed Jones could provide the utopia for which all people strive: happiness, tranquility, and meaningful deeds. Tim Stoen, a graduate of Stanford Law School and a highly respected lawyer in Ukiah, met Jones when Jones served as foreman of the Mendocino County Grand Jury. Stoen joined the church because he saw in the minister "someone who could bring the blacks and whites together in a harmony of love and brotherhood." When asked by a new member why he had joined, Stoen waved his arm around the church and exclaimed, "Just look at all this happiness!"

Michael Prokes, a former TV journalist, revealed: "I joined up because this movement had such ideals." The Bogue family saw Father as "a great humanitarian who would even take in stray dogs and give them medical treatment." Mickey Touchette was attracted because "I felt that Jim Jones was interested in humanitarian qualities . . . no more racism, no more economic inequalities . . . a decent educational system, a decent welfare system." Jeannie Mills became interested because "it appeared that Jim knew how to take care of children."*

One and all built dreams from their own experiences in life, the injustices they had seen and the hard times of which the politicians seemed to know nothing. It was around those dreams that Jones created his "cause." It was their idealism that Jones used to lure them ever deeper into an organized program of total brainwashing and blind captivity.

The American public knew little about brainwashing and mind control before the Korean war and the return

---

* In fact, Jones was using electrodes attached to the arms and legs of children to teach them to smile at the mention of his name.

from North Korea of American POWs with changed personalities. Since then, extensive studies have been made of the phenomenon. Although there are variations in the art of brainwashing, experts agree on six commonly used techniques:

1. Total isolation from the outside world.
2. A rigid daily schedule with absolute obedience to captors.
3. Doctrinaire, daily study groups.
4. Physical abuse, ranging from a lack of food and sleep to beatings and torture.
5. The setting up of criteria by which freedom and approval from the group are contingent on "successful reform."
6. Interrogation sessions in which uncooperative members are grilled and forced to confess, conform, and inform on other members.

Jim Jones employed all six techniques. He began to practice them in Indianapolis, after his return from Father Divine's Peace Mission. Suddenly the personable minister, whom his followers called Jim, announced the Bible full of errors and lies. One Sunday he held the holy book high, then threw it to the floor, shouting, "Too many people are looking at this and not at me!" From then on, the bible was progressively discredited and desecrated, to the point that church members were told to use its pages for toilet paper. Meanwhile, "Jim" suggested, then commanded, that he be called "Father."

At about the same time, Indiana Temple members were puzzled by a newly established "interrogation committee," but when Father explained about "the hidden enemy among us," they went along with the grilling of members who were even the slightest bit critical of him.

Jim Jones knew what kind of people he wanted for his church and systematically recruited them. He also knew that California was the land of the economically and emotionally disenchanted, and he was not the first to recognize the potential in its unorganized numbers. After studying Father Divine's operation on the East Coast, Jones realized instinctively that his land of opportunity was California. In 1965, he headed there with a handful of faithful followers who would serve as a base to expand upon.

In California, Jones gradually but methodically isolated his people. Demanding total loyalty, he had them sever ties with the rest of their families, friends, and outside acquaintances. Except for when they went to work, members had to be accompanied at all times by another member, even to the bathroom. Conversations with strangers were prohibited unless these had been prearranged to suit a People's Temple purpose. The church membership was gripped with a siege mentality that intensified at Jonestown.

In the Guyana jungle, stripped of all identification and unable to leave the armed and guarded compound unless under close surveillance and with the authorization of Jones himself, the people were completely isolated. Other than a harmless visit by the American Embassy once every three to six months, People's Temple was free of government inspection and press inquiry.

There were no newspapers except *People's Forum*, written by Jones and filled with outrageous lies about conditions in the United States (e.g., the city of Los Angeles was abandoned and the Ku Klux Klan was running loose and murdering innocent blacks throughout the country). The only means of communication out of Jonestown was via shortwave radio to the Temple in San Francisco. Not even the most trusted aides were permitted in the radio shack unless Jones was present.

While the minister fortified himself with and became increasingly dependent on amphetamines, he bragged that anybody could function on three hours of sleep a night. After all, he was the perfect example, working twenty-four to thirty-six hours straight. Rhoda Johnson, a sixteen-year-old defector, reported to her Indiana hometown newspaper in 1977 on the exacting daily regime demanded by Jones and his loyal lieutenants in California:

> The pace of living was so strenuous, no one could think straight. My daily schedule was to arise at 6 A.M., go to school until noon, work in a Temple-sponsored restaurant in town until evening, spend the evening working in the nursing home until 10 P.M., then go to church until 3 or 4 A.M. This went on six days a week. The only night I had off was Monday. I never had more than three hours of sleep a night.

The Jonestown daily routine has been discussed already. Twelve-year-old Tracy Parks informed the FBI and the press, shortly after she and her family escaped in one of Congressman Ryan's planes, that Jonestown was "ugly, just like a concentration camp" and that she was forced to stay up until 2 A.M. just to learn lessons like "Russian phrases" before she could eat or go to sleep.

These mandatory doctrinaire study groups became a propaganda barrage that, coupled with no outside contacts, crowded communal conditions, little sleep, little food, hard labor, humiliations, and beatings, greatly affected the thinking processes of his followers. Jim Jones, the orator and con man, quickly progressed from pastor to faith healer to prophet to God. Once his divinity was accepted by the majority of the group, he molded their lives further, using brainwashing techniques.

The people's dependency on Jones intensified as he protected them from the imagined evils of the FBI, KKK,

CIA, and Temple defectors like Jim Cobb. At one California church service, according to Neva Sly, whose husband and son died in Guyana, Jones convinced the congregation that Cobb and his group were making bombs to kill them:

> Jim just went crazy, absolutely crazy. He stood on the podium and started screaming that those kids had gone crazy and that they were in the hills around the church with rifles and that they had stolen money from the church . . . we were totally convinced that there were going to be bombings.

In Jonestown, Father ranted that "the CIA seeded the clouds to make it rain all the time" so they wouldn't have any crops. Their own country and its evil people were inflicting hardships on their agricultural mission because of their revolutionary beliefs. Ironically, he told them that concentration camps were being constructed all along the West Coast. Jim Bogue summed up the feeling of almost everyone in Guyana with Jones: "I was brainwashed by the power of fear." Near the end, using a daily diatribe of lies, exaggerations, and omissions colored with his own intense paranoia, Jones succeeded in making the community fear the outside world much more than their own hellish existence.

All-night meetings, at which members were interrogated and then given the opportunity to confess, became the norm. (Boxes of these written confessions were destroyed by attorney Charles Garry after the massacre.) As important as the confessions were to Jones in controlling would-be defectors and keeping members in line, he had a more immediate method of mind control. Stanley Clayton, a survivor, told how anyone who broke compound rules or who Jones thought wanted to leave was placed in "a large shipping crate 4 feet by 8 feet by 6 feet, for several days to two weeks." This was to "make them totally dependent on others so they could be twisted and turned into what Jones wanted." Michael Prokes, a faithful follower of Jones to the end, confirmed the practice: "The box was in a hole in back of an herbal kitchen by a smokehouse where plantains [similar to bananas] were stored. It was 30 feet by 10 feet and had a smaller box inside." Prokes knew a man who was put in there because he had criticized Jones.

From the beginning, some stronger members resisted Jones' brainwashing by building secret alliances with one another. For example, Jeannie and Al Mills agreed that no matter what happened, they would continue to talk and have sex with each other, which they did, thus preserving their sanity. Realizing this, Jones constantly demanded that members volunteer information on such alliances or face grave punishment. Grace Stoen commented on the critical need to relate to another human being in these circumstances:

> With this alliance, I was able to say to this person: "Hey, there's a beating going on here. Are these real beatings or am I crazy?" This person was able to confirm it—that's how mixed up you were. I mean, you were brainwashed. You were kept up. You got very little sleep. You lacked nutritious food. . . . I was fortunate to have someone, that I could give myself self-assurance that I was not crazy and that I was really seeing what I was seeing.

One of the practices Jones enjoyed most, which was a significant gauge of the effectiveness of the brainwashing, was the beatings. He knew that if he could have his followers beat each other and be beaten, they would be unable to understand or relate realistically to what was happening. Teen-ager Linda Myrtle expressed her feelings and reasons for beating up others in lopsided punishment boxing matches (adults against teen-agers and teen-agers against smaller children:

> I was to carry out the discipline for the boxing. It wasn't a personal thing with me at all. I just was supposed to fight these people for Socialism. And these people, you know, if they did something wrong, I would get into it. The only way I could associate myself . . . or straighten things out in my mind when I was boxing these people . . . was to think about my parents when I was still brainwashed, how they had betrayed Father and the Cause of Socialism; and I would think on that and I would really get outraged and I would be able to fight. . . . It would really give me an extra burst of power, and I would just go off and brutally beat these people, thinking of my parents.

Linda Myrtle severely beat one woman for favoring her own children over the other youngsters. A short time later, Linda was beaten by someone else so badly, she could not sit down for weeks.

> At the time it was right, because I felt what I had done [embraced a friend outside People's Temple gate in San Francisco] was wrong at the time. I was still brainwashed and so confused. I just couldn't rationalize it in my mind that Jim Jones was wrong. I could not say in my mind that he was wrong. I just knew it hurt awfully bad and then, in the end, I had to say, "Thank you, Father," and give him the power sign . . . I felt like I was doing right. Being beaten.

It wasn't until after members had defected that many of them realized they could not cry. Neva Sly recalled:

> We weren't allowed to cry. It was considered a sign of weakness. It was also like we were trying to get sympathy from people. So even if a child was crying and the tears would start in, somebody, but not Jim, but somebody else would always say, "What are you crying for? Are you trying to make us feel sorry for you?" And a lot of people would

jump on the person who was crying, whether it was a child or an adult. It didn't matter at all. So it got to the point where none of us cried.

So effectively did Jones convince his followers that he was God, they inadvertently allowed a young man to die. J. R. Purifoy related how Curtis, who was helping him repair a fire-damaged People's Temple building, overdosed on some kind of drug one night and was found unconscious and near death:

> Instead of them getting him to the hospital to see a doctor, they put a picture of Jones on him to raise him up and heal him. Of course, the child died. Then they took his lifeless body to the hospital and just left it on the front steps. It was a horrible experience. . . . This is how brainwashed the people were, thinking that Jones was God.

Jones broke up families and corrupted and destroyed individuals, and yet, in the strange way of the brainwashed, they clung to their tormentor as their last lifeline. Since he had removed all individual thought process, all drive to succeed or excel, all feeling, all hope, he was all they had left. To the point that Jones was God, he fed that theology with his own rhetoric and prose. The following is a poem he claimed to have written on October 11, 1969:

FOREVER JONES

And from the tomb he did reply:
Tho few have fought so well as I,
Mortal flesh anon must die;
From the depth of skin and bone
Unshaken still, did he intone:
My charges were unloved and lone
And I, destined from the start
To know the grief that storms the heart
of the forsaken and to impart

to them the surging strength of me.
Mightier than the charging sea,
Attuned to all that be, specially unto thee
Who suffered much to walk with me.

Dream ye not of streets of gold.
  Nor an end to pain,
Often in our forever, we will walk
  this way again.

The tall pine opened an aging eye and
  trembled its brittle cones.
Then it fell full length, it did,
  Athwart the tomb of Jones.

> "I've worked hard all my life. My wife gave almost everything we owned to Jim Jones. I've got nothing."
>
> Freddie L. Lewis, a butcher for thirty-four years, who lost his wife, a sister, and seven children at Jonestown

5. Financial Building Blocks of Jones' Empire

The size of Jones' financial empire surprised even his most loyal followers who survived Jonestown. What amounted to a multimillion-dollar operation was built on public welfare and Social Security benefits payable to children and the aged. Under the cloak of religion, Jones, his lawyers, and other advisers devised manipulative, deceitful, and fraudulent methods of collecting these funds and other forms of pension payments due the young and old under his control. By Jones' demanding communal living for his followers, the system was set in place: It was only a matter of time before the members were turning over their incomes, savings, homes, and other means of wealth.

Jim Jones began his ministry in Indianapolis, Indiana, about 1949. For the next sixteen years, amid great controversy, he served his financial apprenticeship. He made mistakes, but also thousands of dollars. The minister, who in his younger days sold imported monkeys door-to-door for $29 apiece, went to California in 1965 with a cashier's check for $100,000, the proceeds from two nursing homes he had operated, taking the patients' Social Security checks and any additional financial assets they had. Members of his church, too, turned over their holdings. Mrs. Esther Mueller sold her home for $25,000 and the furnishings for $2,000, and donated it all to Reverend Jones. The other members were encouraged to follow her example.

In Indiana, Jones formed two corporations for his financial needs. Wings of Deliverance, Inc., was designated a nonprofit, religious, tax-exempt organization for the purpose of receiving funds from the sale of his early real estate acquisitions. Listed as directors for Wings of Deliverance were Jim Jones, his mother, his wife Marceline, and Kathleen Davenport, the People's Temple financial secretary. The second corporation, JIM-LU-MAR, was a profit-making, legal umbrella for the revenue realized from the nursing homes and his wife's income.

As early as 1962, Indiana state licensing authorities started to harass Jones about the poor quality of care in his nursing homes. Without good counseling and because his operations were not legally "clean," he soon ran into trouble with the Internal Revenue Service for failure to pay federal taxes on JIM-LU-MAR. Both corporations eventually had their charters revoked in June 1971.

It was during this period of trouble that Jones shared his vision of "atomic holocaust" with his flock, saying he had read a magazine article on the safest places to live in case of nuclear war. One such was Ukiah, California; another was Belo Horizonte, Brazil. Jones went to Brazil and did missionary work for two years while someone scouted the Ukiah area for him. After the IRS heat cooled down, he returned to Indianapolis to consolidate his holdings and convince his followers that the world would end on July 15, 1967, and the "only place [they] could be safe was with him in California." He left Indiana with his wife, children, and faithful, for a new base of operations in Ukiah.

While getting settled and finding jobs for his Indiana followers, Jones taught another bizarre version of American history, with heavy doses of his sexual philosophy, for several years. He requested and obtained permission for his class size to be appreciably increased. The purpose for such a move was to enable his church members to take his course and thus qualify for increased Social Security benefits. As wage and Social Security checks started to flow again, he formed three new corporations: The Apostolic Corporation and Valley Enterprises, Inc., were nonprofit and tax-exempt, while Truth Enterprises, Inc., served as his profit-making vehicle.

In 1974, on his lawyers' advice, Jones filed a "Certificate of Amendment of Articles of Incorporation of People's Temple of the Disciples of Christ" with the office of Secretary of State, soon to be Governor, Edmund G. Brown, stating, ". . . the specific and primary purpose [of the Temple] is to further the kingdom of God by spreading the Word . . ."

One way specified to spread the divine word, according to the document, was:

> To receive property by devise, or bequest, subject to the laws regulating the transfer of property by will, and otherwise to acquire and hold all property, real or personal,

including, without limitation, shares of stock, bonds, and securities of other corporations . . . To sell, convey, exchange, lease, mortgage, encumber, transfer on trust . . .

The key language of the amendment, however, was point (vii): "To qualify to carry on its non-profit activities in any other state, territory, dependency, or foreign country and to conduct its non-profit activities within or without the State of California." This document was the culmination of the legal paperwork Jones needed to operate within the structure of the law. It enabled him to begin milking his followers and the taxpayers—and to deposit the mounting "religious contributions" in unlimited foreign bank accounts.

As discussed earlier, before Jones began to use legal guardianships to protect himself and divide families, as many as 150 children were channeled through the foster care program into the homes of People's Temple members. Walter Jones, for instance, operated The Jones Family Care Home, and the Touchette family also took in large numbers of children. Some California officials have estimated that Jones could have realized as much as $40,000 a month from that number of foster care children.

These sources of funds, however, were secondary. The most important role of the children was to ensure that their parents remained loyal enough to Jones to turn over all individual assets, present and future, to his cause. In the words of Jim Cobb: "With a religious con man like Jones, you need kids in order to keep a group alive for numbers and for money. If you've got the kids, you've got the parents, and if you've got the parents, you've got the kids."

The children also served an important function by begging for money in the streets of San Francisco, Los Angeles, Ukiah, and, later, Georgetown, Guyana. Denise

Purifoy tells what soliciting was like for the youths of People's Temple:

> They'd send you out with pamphlets of the Temple and a can, and you'd ask everybody you saw for a donation. "Give to the hungry and starving." It was hard . . . they'd give you a certain amount to get, to make, and if you didn't make it, you were in trouble. . . . I never made the quota. Sometimes it'd be $100 . . . the average day was $25 to $30.

According to Linda Myrtle:

> A lot of children were used in the begging technique to raise funds for the Temple because they were adorable . . . you can't say no to a little kid who comes up smiling from ear to ear and says, "Could you please give a donation?" . . . you know. And they were really good at that, little children, so Jim would have most of the adults take a child with them while they were begging.

People's Temple children had seen the "miracles" Jim Jones performed and had heard both their parents and him say he was God. When they begged on the streets, they never took any of the money, for Jones had warned them that if they did, he would know it and punish them severely. One street-wise boy took the chance, however, and stole ten dollars. He waited for Jones' lightning. When nothing happened, he realized they were all being duped, and left the church before the Guyana exodus. His cynicism saved his life.

Jones left no stone unturned. At Sunday Temple collections, plates were replaced with buckets that were passed around as many as seven times in one service. To increase the donations, his aides suggested that Jones himself take the money from worshippers and allow them to touch his robes. The ruse worked.

But trips from San Francisco to Los Angeles with his most loyal members "were worth $15,000 to $20,000 a weekend" in proceeds, according to Grace Stoen. This venture became so lucrative, Jones had a thick armored compartment installed in the back of his bus so that he and the money would be safe for the long ride north.

Young Temple members Theresa Cobb and Mickey Touchette, who spent long hours counting the daily and weekly offerings, told of "mountainous amounts of money" and "high stacks of Social Security and retirement pension-fund checks," which followers dropped in the bucket sooner or later during the fifth, sixth, or seventh passing. After a thorough and successful campaign to pressure members to give up their homes, cars, and other personal possessions, the main source of perpetual revenue for Jim Jones was these checks. In 1972, he explained to Jeannie Mills and other close staff his willingness to take so many older people into the membership:

> They serve several functions that will be very helpful to us in the future. First, if we are ever trying to escape into another country, the border guards will see all our old people and assume that we are a humanitarian group. Also, no border guard would want to detain buses that are loaded with elderly people who might have heart attacks or strokes. But more importantly, if we are ever to relocate in another country, these people's Social Security and pension checks would follow them. In a communal situation in another country, where the cost of living is lower, our entire group might be able to survive on these checks until we are able to find other means of making money.

Six years later, after the massacre, a search of Jones' private quarters revealed a trunkful of passports and 656 uncashed Social Security checks. These checks, payments for the period July–October 1978 to some 199 Social Security "annuitants" living in the People's Temple Agricultural Mission, totaled $160,000.

On December 11, 1978, Representative Clement J. Zablocki of the House Foreign Affairs Committee wrote to the Health, Education, and Welfare Secretary, Joseph Califano, asking his cooperation in "sharing any information your department has on the alleged theft or fraudulent use of Social Security payments to members of the People's Temple in the United States or Guyana." Three months later, on March 7, 1979, the Secretary of HEW responded with his departmental interim review: "The report indicates that, to date, no basis has been found for concluding that the People's Temple stole or fraudulently used Social Security benefits received by its members."

However, privileged information from People's Temple files, radio communications between Jonestown and San Francisco, and sources within the Department of Social Security Administration give a very different picture from that painted by official Washington. Jones' Social Security scam was so lucrative that by February 1977, the small western branch of the Social Security office in San Francisco had to assign a full-time employee to work exclusively on the claims and financial maneuvers of People's Temple.

Generally speaking, there are two types of Social Security benefits for children, as well as for adults. The first is commonly referred to as "gold" because the checks are gold-colored. These benefits come from Supplemental Security Income (SSI), a form of federal welfare for children and adults who cannot work because of blindness, mental retardation, or other kinds of disability. Some legal guardians were permitted to draw SSI checks on the Social Security numbers of their public wards for as much as $280 a month, most of which was then remitted to People's Temple.

The second type of benefit, the "green" checks, is

derived from retirement funds after sixty-two, survival benefits, and so forth. The amount of money depends on how much the worker has paid into the system during his or her employment years. According to sources in Washington, some Temple children were getting benefits on their parents' accounts, part of which was sent to Guyana.

The Social Security Act (43 U.S.C. 407) provides that "the right of any person to any future payment under this title shall not be transferable or assignable, at law or in equity . . ." However, Jim Jones, a master at deluding the system, circumvented the law and the Social Security officials with his "communal living for young and old" under the religious umbrella of the People's Temple Church.

Gradually but systematically, Jones established his communal-living setup. Children were taken away from their natural parents either through the courts or through the minister's power of persuasion. Almost the entire San Francisco membership ended up living in communes and handing over all paychecks and Social Security and welfare payments to the church. In turn, they received a two-dollar weekly allowance, which was usually donated back to the church under the watchful eye of Reverend Jones and his rhetorical appeals for the poor.

Bonnie Purifoy lived with thirteen other people in a three-bedroom trailer and slept on the floor most of the time. Linda Myrtle remembered the single room she shared in the Temple with fourteen other women and a small baby: "There were rats in the building, and at night, mice and rats and everything would run over the rug and over me when I was asleep. I would awake and couldn't sleep." Yet the total income for these 15 women, from outside work and begging, amounted to about $68,000 a year. Jackie Colbert, a foster child for ten years, recalled seeing the "checks for foster care go straight to Jones."

Forty-nine people were registered as occupants of 1029 Geary Street. So many gold and green checks were being sent there that the curiosity of officials at the regional Social Security office was aroused. Apparently nothing "unlawful" was ever found, however, even though the commune netted Jones an approximate monthly income of over $22,000.

In January 1977, by printing "authorization representative forms," Jones attempted to have all SSI and SSA checks flow directly into one account at the Montreal Bank in San Francisco. Hundreds signed over their SSI and SSA benefits to People's Temple, thus breaking the law. Officials then challenged People's Temple by saying that all the individual checks couldn't be put into one account.

In October 1977, the Social Security office in San Francisco assigned Robert Stone to handle the People's Temple account. Jim Jones appointed his trusted aide Jim Randolph to work with Stone. By law, the SSA representative had to check on recipients and "redetermine" if they were still eligible for SSI support. A former official of People's Temple told how Stone would be handled for his redetermination visits:

> Jones would always outnumber him by six or seven people, who had been instructed to sit in chairs higher than the investigator's. Any forms Stone requested to be signed were taken to the person [said to be in the next room] and returned, without the federal official ever really knowing if anyone was in the next room or not. Stone's requests for face-to-face meetings were ignored to the point where he stopped asking.

Stone never did see the signees, and to this day, the legality of Social Security payments to most Temple members is questionable.

Stone's reports, however, made the west San Francisco office of Social Security very wary of Jones. When People's Temple hastily moved to Guyana and Jones and his staff failed to have eligible members fill out Form SSA 21 (required of annuitants leaving the country), the San Francisco Social Security Administration stopped the payments. After three or four months, Jones became incensed over the loss of income and started a massive letter-writing campaign to the White House. The White House turned the complaint over to the Division of Sensitive Inquiries at the Division of International Operations of Social Security in Baltimore, Maryland. "We felt the heat," said Stu Brown of that office, and so the flow of checks resumed to finance communal living at Jonestown, Guyana.

Illuminating Jones' orchestrated use of Social Security benefits were the recorded messages from the People's Temple radio transmitter (WB6-MNH/8RI). The following is an example of communications between Randolph and Jones, and between Randolph, Carolyn Layton, the Temple's financial wizard, and attorney Eugene Chaikin:

Randolph to Jones:

We have caught several checks that came to old addresses . . . Eventually we will collect all benefits that people are eligible to, but it will take longer.

He then talked about discontinued SSI checks because the beneficiary had left the country:

. . . should we keep all those we are eligible to whether sent out or deposited directly in the bank?

. . . how are we to go about cashing them?

. . . I am enclosing all the checks I have on hand to which we are eligible. Some need to be endorsed.

Randolph to Layton and Chaikin:

We plan to hang on to all SSI checks rather than return them so long as technical eligibility exists—even though we don't know how we will be cashing them, and even though they are the notorious gold checks. I have already returned several, thinking there was no eligibility, a mistake I won't repeat!

In April 1978, Stone told Randolph to have SSI annuitants who were out of the country return their checks. A worried Randolph radioed Jonestown:

I got instructions to return the SSI checks individually . . . I will simply address an envelope for each person who has checks to return. No cover letter of explanation, no return address, no return receipt requested [and therefore no receipt of the contents]. I will just mail them to the respective district offices. I am a little worried because some of them are already endorsed.

What is important here is the fact that occupants had started arriving in Jonestown in the summer of 1977. Yet almost a year later, Robert Stone was ordering the return of SSI (gold) checks because it was a violation of the law for persons to be out of the country and still receiving them.

On February 2, 1979, California State Social Services Director Marion Woods asserted that his department had found "at least twenty-eight cases of welfare fraud involving People's Temple members who received welfare payments after they were in Guyana." He also cited 142 cases of Temple members who were obtaining combined state/federal program funds administered by the federal Social Security Administration.

Jones instructed his staff to do an "income survey" on the people leaving the United States so that, later, People's Temple could apply for additional benefits in Guyana. That survey prompted the following radio message on Valentine's Day, 1978.

> There are some miscellaneous notes from the income survey . . . you might discuss . . . going through some kind of accreditation procedure which would ultimately result in our being recognized by Social Security so kids eligible for SSA benefits when in school can receive those benefits while there:
>
> Mark Boutte—eligible for SSA if in an accredited school.
> Carol Ann Kerns—used to get $60 a month from father as support. Would he give her anything as a student?
> Kay Rosas—SSA was discontinued following her marriage to some guy to keep him from going to Vietnam. Grounds for annulment? Benefits might be forthcoming if she were single again.
> Janice Wilsey—eligible to any BIA [Bureau of Indian Affairs] money?
> Eddie Dennis—heavy-equipment operator. Norris Industry. Union retirement?
> Mary Griffith—might be eligible because worked ten years prior to leaving U.S.; also on deceased husband's claim.
> Lemuel Thomas—has he actually received money from State Teachers Retirement System?
> Robert Kice—did he receive a pension from Masonite?
> Dorothy Sanders—has retirement coming from the Post Office. Being worked on from here.
> Martha Souder—anything due her because she was married to and divorced from ILWU worker?

Flawless records were kept for every conceivable avenue of revenue. The "income survey" files comprehensively listed both possible and definite sources of income. For instance, Millie Cunningham had four listed: "SSA, SSI, Bank, and V.A."; Eugenia Gernandt had five listed: "SSA, SSI, Bank, V.A., and State Retirement Fund"; and Edna Reed (who displeased them by not reporting her job): "SSA . . . and *Job* (didn't report)." Handwritten notes next to all the names being processed for travel to Guyana summarized how much these people were currently receiving in benefits: "Little Najauandrienne Darnes—$111"; "L. B. Rheeves—$239 and $223 for children"; "Don Jackson—Disability, $430."

After most of the members left for Guyana, Social Security officials noticed that all the SSA (green) checks were being sent to a common post office box number. U.S. Consul Richard McCoy visited Jonestown three times; his successor, Douglas Ellice, and Vice Consul Dennis Reece also checked into the matter. McCoy reported, paradoxically, that although he found "Social Security beneficiaries who were heavily influenced to turn over their monthly benefits to the Temple . . . these individuals voluntarily gave their money to the Temple and appeared to be adequately housed, fed, and in relatively good health." The officials were convinced that "the post office box address was being used for the convenience of the beneficiaries . . . and . . . that each annuitant interviewed was receiving and controlling the use of his monthly payment and that none had assigned his checks to the Temple." Therefore, the SSA office saw no reason to discontinue "the procedure of mailing the monthly checks to the Jonestown post office box address."

The above findings were part of the May 15, 1979, report of the Staff Investigative Group to the House Foreign Affairs Committee on "The Assassination of Representative Leo J. Ryan and the Jonestown, Guyana, Tragedy." The same report, under "Role and Performance of the U.S. Department of State," also stated: "It is proven beyond doubt that Jones staged a show for selective visitors to Jonestown which made it difficult to get a realistic and accurate picture of what was actually happening there . . ."

It went on to say that the Embassy consul in Georgetown advised Jones far in advance who was coming to the compound, whom they wanted to see, and why. Before their arrival, the proper Temple people were sufficiently "coached" on what to do and say. No visitors were ever permitted into the crowded living quarters of the residents.

Except for those who were very loyal to Jim Jones or who had positions of privilege, the vast majority of the people lived in fear and terror and had to work long, hard hours in the fields and various workshops in Jonestown. On one occasion, United Stated officials visited the compound to see if members who were receiving retirement benefits were, in fact, working and therefore not eligible for Social Security. They were assured that these people were enjoying their hobbies and not working at all.

Vern Gosney, who escaped when Congressman Ryan was about to leave but whose five-year-old son was murdered, complained that whenever the visiting consular officials from the American Embassy in Georgetown came to Jonestown, they were kept away from everyone except the public relations staff, who showed them only what Jones wanted them to see. Gosney also said that on the day of his arrival at Jonestown, the minister's armed guards told him he would never "leave this place alive."

Jonestown was the final communal-living design, conceived by Jones not as a human experiment in living and growing, but as a devious plan to lure and trap people, and to direct their modest streams of dollars into a river of millions to be stored in foreign bank reservoirs. It is now estimated that even before the exodus to Guyana, People's Temple was receiving an average of $250,000 a month from its many sources of income.

In an interview, Tim Stoen told how Jones had asked him to develop a "concept of concealment" for the increasing amounts of cash flowing into the coffers: "Tim, set up a scheme whereby we can get our assets protected, and do it in a legitimate way." Stoen obliged by creating a "Temple branch" in Luxembourg. From there, accounts were opened in London, West Germany, Switzerland, Romania, Panama, and Venezuela. Jim Jones, a self-styled Marxist, had a personal account opened under a dummy corporation named "Bridget." According to one of the few trusted aides who could sign for bank transactions, the initial deposit in this account was $1.5 million.

The estimated, reported wealth of People's Temple—$26 million—still scattered among foreign banks and now the object of billions of dollars in legal claims, came from the small incomes and savings of thousands of trusting people. The children begged on the streets; Jones begged from his pulpit. His members, mesmerized by his oratorical skills, exchanged their modest financial holdings for his grandiose promise of a revolutionary cause that would grant them all a better life. Giving up whatever financial security they had, and without a source of income, they sealed their fate.

> "He . . . exploited the children unmercifully in his political machine. They were required to sit up hours and hours and hours and write letters. They would take telephone directories and write letters in people's names out of the directories. They would take the letters that they had written and mail them all up and down the whole state of California, like they were coming from different parts of the state. The children were his labor and work force."
>
> J. R. Purifoy, former member of People's Temple

6. Politics + Public Relations = Power

Saturday evening, November 18, 1978, Dr. Carlton Goodlett, a physician, the publisher of the Oakland *Sun Reporter,* and a powerful voice in the black community of northern California, was dining with friends at a private home with a beautiful view of San Francisco Bay. The phone rang twice that evening, and Dr. Goodlett's world fell apart.

The caller was San Francisco Mayor George Moscone. Frantically, he informed his friend that People's Temple in San Francisco had just told him it had received unconfirmed reports, via shortwave from Guyana, that Congressman Leo Ryan and his investigating party had been ambushed and killed. Reverend Jim Jones and his followers also were killing themselves at that very moment.

Goodlett, personal physician, close friend, and strong supporter of Jim Jones, was visibly shaken and refused to believe what he had heard. He asked Mayor Moscone to do some further checking on what had to be a preposterous rumor. In the second call, the mayor confirmed the unbelievable, and they both "broke down and cried like babies."

It was symbolic that these two men—one a powerful city politician and the other a prominent newspaper publisher—heard the news and shared the grief together. Dr. Goodlett and Mayor Moscone were key members of the coalition Jones had built to enhance his own political power base—a base initiated in Mendocino County and perfected in San Francisco, from which he rose to impressive heights. Using slick public relations and cleverly duping the press, Jones gained the reputation of a humanitarian whose religious works were dedicated to helping the poor and uplifting society's failures. In fact, he was a power broker, with an army of political workers who, at his command, would march for his choice of potential politicians or elected office holders.

Without question, Jones hoodwinked the politicians. In keeping with the ritual of American politics, the power moguls, including Governor Jerry Brown and Mrs. Jimmy Carter, heaped praise on this man of whom they knew literally only one thing—that he could provide a host of dedicated, tireless campaign workers. As the children labored in the "grass roots," far removed from the eyes of the public and the candidates, Jones built a reputable powerhouse. From its center he weathered major assaults from defectors who, knowing the truth, battered its ramparts in vain to save their loved ones.

Jones' influence peddling began in the summer of 1965, when a black Cadillac pulled into Ukiah, which was to be his first California base. In the car was Jones, his wife, Marceline, and their interracial family of four children. Armed with information his Ukiah scout had gleaned for him while he himself was in Brazil, Jones arrived with a plan to completely dominate the area that he claimed would "provide safety from nuclear fallout." The townspeople never knew what hit them.

With efficient speed, the minister found employment for the busload of 100 loyal followers from Indianapolis who had uprooted their lives and livelihoods to remain close to their god. Soon, every key office in the local and county governments had a People's Temple member employed and reporting back to Jim Jones. With objectives similar to those of a military operation, they penetrated and controlled or neutralized basic community departments and communications.

The *Ukiah Daily Journal* was an important but easy target. Jones provided its editor with a free houseworker and nurse for his ailing wife. When the editor's daughter-in-law had her first baby, Reverend Jones paid the hospital bill and later supplied the man with a young, attractive receptionist—Maria Katsaris. The publisher of the *Journal* was most appreciative for the many ads Jones brought to the paper: The two established a congenial relationship from which flowed a series of complimentary stories on Jones, the dedicated altruist. Since the *Journal* was the only newspaper in the area, Jones had effectively counterchecked future critics.

People's Temple began building a massive promotional campaign. Pictures of adorable children graced the brochures, handouts, and press releases. Smiling innocents, with the right touch of "religious connotation"—"Whatever measure you use to give, large or small, will be used to measure what is given back to you": Luke 6:30—lent heart-robbing appeal to financial solicitations that filled mailbags, which in turn filled mail trucks and eventually filled Jones' bank accounts.

It was during this time, too, that hundreds of children and senior citizens were packed into buses, and the "Caravan of Hope" began its 10,000-mile, three-week trip across the country, attracting glowing editorial comments on their behavior and performance. In addition to their own literature, church members handed out a booklet entitled *Family Council on Crime Resistance,* excellent for families coping with crime, but hypocritical in its objective: Jones was criminally destroying the family fibers of his own following.

With the public relations campaign in full swing, Jones simultaneously developed a political machine worthy of the envy of any politician. Again, the children and senior citizens formed the vital nucleus. Ukiah-Redwood Valley, in Mendocino County, provided their basic training. One of the people to benefit was Mrs. Wayne Boynton, then chairman of the Mendocino County Republican Party, of which Jones was a member. Mrs. Boynton talked with the *Los Angeles Times* after the massacre:

> They [Temple membership] were a dream come true. They would do precinct work. They would get information from the courthouse. They would do the grubbies—addressing envelopes, making phone calls. They'd do anything you'd ask, and so quickly you couldn't believe it.

According to children and parents interviewed by this writer, Mrs. Boynton's work was completed in record time because Jones forced the children and adults to stay up all night to do it.

Fifteen-year-old Linda Myrtle described the mandatory work done by young "volunteers" for one candidate Jones was supporting: "We would leave school and go to the Wirth headquarters and man the phones and ask people were they going to vote for Congressman Wirth. And if they said no, or whatever, we'd write it down."

A father whose four children were drafted into the workings of the Temple's political machine stated: "He [Jones] exploited the children unmercifully in his political activities. Using the telephone directory, the kids would spend endless hours copying down names and writing letters for candidates."

Other political chores included passing out leaflets the day before election and going door-to-door for Jones' chosen candidates.

Year-round, for young and old, Wednesday was letter-writing night, and everyone had to work a minimum of six hours. Jim Cobb described the technique as he remembered it during his teens in People's Temple: "We would look at telephone books and get a first name here and a last name there and make up false names." Richard D. Tropp, who won a Woodrow Wilson Fellowship and had dreams of becoming a writer, headed up the letter-writing committee. Each person was given a copy of a letter Tropp had composed and an instruction sheet for variations of the draft letter. The following instruction sheet applied to a letter addressed to then Vice President Nelson Rockefeller.

SPECIAL LETTER TO GO OUT—EVERYONE MUST WRITE

Write a short letter thanking Vice-President Rockefeller for giving such a superb speech. Our Pastor, Jim Jones, thinks so very much of you (respects you, etc.) and appreciated all that you said at the Religion in American Life dinner the other night. Some—say that Pastor Jones told you about his great speech.

You can also say things like:

- —I think you are a great Vice-President.
- —I wish you the best of success.
- —All of our members at People's Temple Christian Church think the world of you.
- —We need leaders like you in these times.
- —Pastor Jones has always taught us to appreciate and respect governmental leaders, and has praised you often for your concern for people, etc.
- —It is important to see leaders in government taking an interest in (and honoring) our nation's religious leaders.
- —We've looked to you often for wisdom and guidance and have found you to be a tremendous inspiration.
- —I want you to know that whoever Pastor Jim Jones respects, I respect. And he thinks the world of you. You have done so much for the country, and for the office of the Vice-President
- —You have shown courage and wisdom in so many issues, etc.

Do not seal your letter. Please have it done by tomorrow night's meeting. It can be short. Put it in a stamped envelope, and address it to:

> Vice-President Nelson Rockefeller
> Washington, D.C.

Put your return address on the letter. Use a previous address if you wish. Some can use a variation on this address—say Vice-President Rockefeller, *or* Nelson A. Rockefeller. Some can put on his address Office of the Vice-President, or Vice-President of the United States.

Other projects of People's Temple were constant, consistent reminders to the political machine that Jones was essential to its success:

1. The Temple bakery turned out cakes for the bereaved survivors listed in the daily obituary columns.
2. Telephone banks were set up before elections. Temple members called registered voters and solicited their votes for Jones' hand-picked candidates.
3. Children and adults canvassed door-to-door before the election, using the personal approach to get out the vote for the Temple's selected candidate.
4. Little children, particularly, worked long, hard hours passing out campaign literature. Called adorable by the voters, they were most effective.
5. People's Temple contributed sizable sums so that the candidates would not forget.
6. Jones supported both slates or candidates without either side's knowledge. That way, he was always the winner.
7. Finally, People's Temple Church served as a large and enthusiastic forum to feed the egos of candidates.

With political wars come the spoils, and Jones knew exactly what he wanted. Important jobs in sensitive governmental departments (Mendocino County Welfare Department, the office of the district attorney, the sheriff's office, the Police Dispatch Unit) became increasingly available to People's Temple members. Strategically placed, these people monitored their offices and departments and reported anything that hinted of potential trouble for Jones. It is small wonder that when teacher Ruby Bogner, who had filed a threat and harassment charge against People's Temple, inquired years later about the outcome of the charge, she was told that no record of such a complaint existed.

The patronage system so effectively isolated Jones from governmental scrutiny that he was awarded high public profile appointments—foremanship of the Mendocino County Grand Jury and a seat on the County Juvenile Justice and Delinquency Prevention Board. These posts gave him a public platform from which he generated additional publicity. The publicity, in turn, provided him with more recruits for his church, and the increasing membership gained him more workers, more control, and more power.

With virtually total conquest of the communities of Ukiah and Redwood Valley, Jones began to recruit talent to serve his designs for expanded political action, massive public relations, and legal protection. San Francisco was his talent-draft choice. The minister knew that the volatile 1960s, with the Civil Rights upsurge, three assassinations, the Vietnam war, and the drug culture, had burned out many young people. He also realized that the San Francisco Bay Area was a magnet for disenchanted idealists. Combining charm and revolutionary rhetoric, he captivated some young, very bright minds and enlisted them to help him lead People's Temple into the 1970s.

The purchase of a fleet of buses gave his public relations "army" rapid mobility as he enlarged his weekend services to both Los Angeles and San Francisco. During the early forays, he and his lieutenants visited local church services and rated the ministers' performances. He also met with San Francisco politicians, evaluated their strengths and weaknesses, and made index cards on them for future use. These early days of scouting and reporting formed the basis for his overall strategy and actions in that city.

After six years of solid growth and political muscle-testing in Mendocino County, Jones was ready for the move to San Francisco. In the spring of 1971, a long line of buses and cars left Redwood Valley and transferred the People's Temple central operation to a new location on Geary Street in the Fillmore district—the heart of the black community—of San Francisco.

Almost overnight, the Temple's propaganda program was in full operation. In the tradition of Father Divine, Pastor Jim offered free meals, good health care, and convincing oratory on social justice. Realizing that his "good works" would attract members of black churches in the Fillmore district, Jones and his aides devised a plan to overcome the expected bitter opposition from black clergymen. The strategy was to win the confidence of one man: Carlton B. Goodlett, Ph.D., M.D., president of the National Newspaper Publishers Association and a leading figure in the black community, who had once run for governor against former Governor Edmund G. "Pat" Brown, and whose political views were "pro-Marxist socialism."

Dr. Goodlett already had been profiled and categorized by People's Temple staff, and Jones knew Dr. Goodlett long before the black leader had ever heard of Jim Jones. Starting with his quarry's name on a small 3 by 5 index card, Jones charmed his way into the man's heart and confidence. Goodlett would become his personal physician, his friend, and his defender in death.

As Jones predicted, the Fillmore clergymen were threatened by the inroads he was making into their memberships. During this crucial period, they formed a delegation to talk to Dr. Goodlett about the "white intruder." After listening to their complaints, Goodlett offered this advice:

> Listen, this man (Jones) looks to me like he's pretty successful in interpreting the functional gospel. I don't know what brand of whiskey he drinks, but if he drinks a special brand of whiskey, you better drink it yourselves.

So impressed was Goodlett with Jones that any time public criticism was leveled at People's Temple or its pastor, the publisher would place his respected newspaper at Jones' disposal to defend himself.

Goodlett was not the only member of the press seduced by Jones and his apparent good works. *San Francisco Chronicle* columnist Herb Caen wrote glowing accolades on People's Temple, and Steve Gavin, city editor of the *San Francisco Examiner,* attended Temple services and a testimonial dinner for the minister. Even after the Jonestown massacre, Gavin told Jeannie Kasindorf of *New West Magazine:*

> [Jones] was a very exciting, very impressive person who said all the right things . . . possibly the most fascinating person I've ever met. He invited me to the service and it was a real high, this joyous kind of feeling of love and caring for each other.

Jones' overtures to the press were effective for the first six years in San Francisco. His public image grew with each new article on his amazingly innovative drug abuse program, lunches for senior citizens, and crime prevention programs for youths. The newspapers reported everything the minister wanted in print, including his $500 donation to the family of California Highway Patrol Officer Al Turner, who was shot on the job, and a People's Temple contribution of $4,400 "in defense of the press."

In January 1973, the *San Francisco Chronicle* accepted $500 from Jones' "Free Press Fund" in good faith. In an article expressing his thanks, the publisher, Charles deYoung Thieriot, described People's Temple for his readers:

> Called less formally PT, the church is best known and highly regarded for its social works, which include housing and feeding senior citizens and medical convalescents,

maintaining a home for retarded boys, rehabilitating youthful drug users and assisting non-members as well as members of the faith through college and legal difficulties.

So within eighteen months of opening the new church on Geary Street, Jones could comfortably count on the support of and promotion from local media. He also knew the exact needs of the politicians. He and his workers, dubbed "the troops," soon became an awesome commodity in political circles. Said one high Democratic State Committee staff person, "They were made to order. You should have seen it—old ladies on crutches, whole families, little kids . . ." Jones was noted for his ability to turn out a crowd of 2,000 with only a six-hour notice.

The minister's public relations plan also called for the infiltration of other influential organizations with media and political connections. While going through the San Francisco Temple Church with *NBC News,* this writer found a NAACP membership card for Larry Layton (who has been tried in Guyana for his role in the shooting of Congressman Ryan and others). Layton was one of 300 members of People's Temple for whom Jones paid the ten-dollar membership dues in the NAACP. They literally took over the local branch, and shortly thereafter, Jones was elected to the board of directors. A similar move was made to take over the Black Leadership Forum in San Francisco, but an astute change in the bylaws by its membership saved that organization.

At the same time, an internal master plan was devised for use in discrediting any critics of People's Temple, whether defectors or investigators from the media or government. The plan was called "Diversions Department" and operated as described in Jim Cobb's lawsuit against Jones:

A. *Defectors & Critics Division:* To divert individual persons, particularly ex-members of People's Temple and outspoken critics thereof, from publicizing and from organizing in opposition to the practices of defendants JONES and PEOPLE'S TEMPLE, by threatening such persons with death and injury to their persons and properties, including threats that their homes will be burned;

B. *Government & Media Division:* To divert agencies of government and of the media from investigating the practices of defendants JONES and PEOPLE'S TEMPLE by:

(1). "Bombarding" them with continual mass volumes of letters written in longhand by People's Temple members conscripted as part of "letter-writing committees" which allege various types of unjustified harassment; and

(2). Making anonymous telephone calls to agencies of government and the media, which accuse totally innocent persons selected at random of heinous crimes and immoral acts (particularly crimes and acts related to those for which defendant JONES feared he was about to be accused); and

C. *General Public Division:* To divert the public from focusing upon the questionable practices of defendants JONES and PEOPLE'S TEMPLE by publishing press releases and other communications which falsely accuse the critics of such practices as being sexual deviates, terrorists, drug traffickers or child molesters.

The operation was used liberally in general, but most extensively against Tim Stoen after he defected and joined forces with the Concerned Relatives. A People's Temple letter to the U.S. Agency for International Development charged: "The Stoens instigated his [Jones] relationship with Grace, over Tim's pleas to protect his reputation from embarrassment of threatened exposure of his transvestite patterns."

The coalition Jones built between political leaders and the media gave him an unassailable position in the power structure of San Francisco up to the mid-1970s. His army of political "volunteers" were used to support whomever he wished to put in office. To the powerful weapons at his command was added another—fear. As word spread that Jones wouldn't hesitate to discredit or destroy anyone who got in his way or crossed him or his cause, more and more politicians felt uneasy about him.

The years 1975 and 1976 were his political zenith. In 1975, George Moscone ran for mayor and Joe Freitas for district attorney. Jones threw his workers—children, teen-agers, and elderly—behind the two men, and they both won very tight races—Moscone by a mere 4,000 votes and Freitas by about 9,000. The closeness of these elections gave Jones significant new leverage, prompting State Assemblyman Willie Brown's assessment: "In a tight race like the ones that George and Joe had, forget it without Jones." Jones was rewarded with the appointment to chairmanship of the city's Housing Authority, and Tim Stoen, then his trusted lawyer, joined the staff of District Attorney Freitas.

With this high public profile, more awards began to come, some of them engineered by Jones and his staff. In April 1975, he was named "one of the 100 most outstanding clergymen in the nation" by Religion in American Life, Inc., an interfaith organization. Dr. Goodlett's newspaper, the *Sun Reporter,* presented him with a "Citizen's Merit Award" for his dedication to social justice. And in January 1976, a most coveted award, "Humanitarian of the Year," was bestowed on Pastor Jones by the *Los Angeles Herald*. This award gave People's Temple a platform from which to boast of its generous financial support to worthy causes and organizations: the Fresno Bee Newsmen, the Telegraph-Hill

Medical Clinic, American Cancer Society, Mendocino County Heart Association, Sickle-Cell Anemia Testing Program, Educational Broadcasting Stations, Big Brothers of America; and to antihunger groups: Bread for the World, North of Market Senior Escort Program, and even the Police Fishing Program.

While all this was merely token support to further build Jones' credibility in the Bay Area, it paid off when state Democratic officials solicited his help with a scheduled visit from Rosalyn Carter, who was campaigning for her husband's successful bid for the Presidency. Jones had already figured prominently in campaign functions for Lieutenant Governor Mervyn Dymally, Governor Jerry Brown, Tom Hayden (husband of actress Jane Fonda), and others.

In retrospect, Mrs. Carter's visit to San Francisco on September 14, 1976, was not one of the Secret Service's finest hours. The rally for the future First Lady was held at a Market Street storefront serving as the Democratic campaign headquarters for Jimmy Carter. People's Temple buses parked behind the store after depositing the children and elderly, who strategically filled the front rows of chairs. Jones arrived with a score of armed bodyguards, some of whom were convicted felons with records of aggravated assault.

The United States Secret Service worked hand in hand with Jones' security force, searching the area for bombs and "suspicious characters who may be armed." At one point, a bodyguard of Jones' pointed to a man he suspected of carrying a weapon. The Secret Service agent duly approached and searched the man. At the same time, a Democratic official spotted a gun on one of Jones' bodyguards and voiced his concern to the Secret Service, but was told it was "OK."

Since the audience was packed with People's Temple

members, Jones received more applause than anyone, including Mrs. Carter. She and her advance team were most impressed and pleased with Jones and the enthusiastic turnout. She readily agreed to his request for a private audience later in the day.

That evening, Jones pulled into the prestigious Stanford Court Hotel's courtyard in a chauffeured limousine, followed by two other cars. To the amazement of the Carter people and the Secret Service, Jones entered the hotel with at least a dozen armed bodyguards in dress suits. It took some intense reassuring and quiet but firm maneuvering by the Carter advance team to separate the guards from Jones.

No one knows precisely what was discussed, but close aides to the minister reported that the Guyana project and Carter's campaign in California were priority subjects. Apparently, a mutually satisfactory agreement was reached, for shortly afterward, 200 to 250 "volunteers" from People's Temple turned up to work for the Central Committee's "Get-Out-The-Vote" drive for Carter. According to party officials, the Temple youths and senior citizens made up more than 10 percent of the entire state's campaign volunteer effort.

On September 25, 1976, eleven days after Mrs. Carter's entourage left San Francisco, the Establishment turned out en masse to honor Reverend Jim Jones at his church. The guest list was a political spectrum, from the chairman of the Republican Party in Mendocino County to leading Democrats in San Francisco. There was Angela Davis on the far left, and a leading member of the John Birch Society on the far right. In between were all the important politicians, media, and civic personalities of the city: Lieutenant Governor Mervyn Dymally, State Senator Milton Marks, Mayor George Moscone, District Attorney Joseph Freitas, Supervisor Robert Mendelsohn,

Police Chief Charles Gain, Dr. Goodlett of the *Sun Reporter*, Steve Gavin of the *San Francisco Chronicle*, and members of the Gay Movement.

As the children of People's Temple unobtrusively provided entertainment and served food, State Assemblyman Willie Brown, the master of ceremonies, added another jewel of praise to the cult leader's promotional crown:

> Jim Jones is a rare, rare, rare specimen. Jim Jones is a symbol of what we all ought to be about... Jim Jones is, in my opinion, a true human being. Let me present to you what you should see every day when you look into the mirror in the early morning hours. Let me present to you a combination of Martin Luther King, Angela Davis, Albert Einstein, Chairman Mao...

The crowd roared its approval with a standing ovation.

With an eye on expanding horizons, Jim Jones also sought public approval by national leaders. The Temple's files show endorsements from, among others, the late Hubert H. Humphrey, Jane Fonda, and Roy Wilkins. (This respectability later proved very costly to the parents who, fighting to free their children from the cult, were rebuffed and neutralized in their efforts.)

> The work of Reverend Jones and his congregation is testimony to the positive and truly Christian approach to dealing with the myriad problems confronting our society today.
>
> Hubert H. Humphrey

> During this period when there are such serious problems with which our minorities are faced, it is encouraging to learn that there is such an effective effort which is being made by the People's Temple.
>
> Roy Wilkins

Much of what America needs to resolve its overwhelming social problems has become embodied into the life of Jim Jones and the works of People's Temple.

Jane Fonda

Reverend Jim Jones has been a friend to hundreds of youth in the city, and his church has rehabilitated many from drug use, helped young people out of legal difficulty and antisocial patterns . . . His church has taken . . . children abandoned by parents and unwanted by agencies.

Joseph E. Hall
NAACP, San Francisco branch

Ninety-nine percent of all the work done by People's Temple is in service to the elderly, poor families, and troubled youth . . . It is most unfortunate that some people . . . feel threatened by this simple organization and philosophy of service.

Art Agnos, majority whip
California State Assembly

I am grateful . . . for . . . the work of the People's Temple Christian Church in defending the First Amendment guarantees of freedom of the press . . . and in running the ranch for handicapped children.

Walter F. Mondale

I say without qualification that this church has been second to none in preventing crime . . . They have donated thousands of dollars to city-sponsored fund drives for the purpose of creating summer jobs for youth and programs for cultural enrichment. They have sent some of their wayward youth to their large agricultural mission in South America entirely at their own cost.

Joe Johnson, former deputy mayor
City of San Francisco

At different times when Vice President Mondale and Attorney General Griffin Bell visited San Francisco, Jim Jones was invited to meet with Mondale on Air Force

One and with Bell at a private dinner at the home of the influential lawyer Robert Wallach. Now the reverend's political clout spanned the nation—from a black ghetto on the West Coast to the White House and the halls of the Justice Department in Washington.

Amidst the adulation for Jim Jones from the uninformed and the compromised, a handful of inquisitive reporters had their doubts. As far back as 1972, Lester Kinsolving, religious editor for the *San Francisco Examiner*, prepared a series of articles on the minister. Two installments—"The Prophet Who Raises the Dead" and "Healing Prophet Hailed as God"—were published before management buckled under a barrage of letters and phone calls and nonstop picketing by People's Temple children and adults. The picketing got extensive TV and newspaper coverage. However, not one reporter questioned why the children, who marched all day without a rest or lunch, were not in school. No mention was made, either, of the children's dinner of dry peanut butter sandwiches (partially frozen) and a small drink of Kool-Aid while they continued to march.

In 1977, Gordon Lindsay, of the *National Enquirer*, also wrote an exposé on Jones, but threats of libel action made the national weekly decide not to run it. Marshall Kilduff, of the *San Francisco Examiner*, was more tenacious when he asked his editor, Steve Gavin, if he could look into People's Temple. Gavin, by his own admission, was impressed with Jones and did not give his reporter permission to investigate either the church or its leader, who by now was constantly surrounded by armed guards and refused to be interviewed.

Kilduff took his story concept to *New West Magazine*, where senior editor Kevin Starr liked the idea for an investigative piece and gave the young reporter the green light. It was not an easy assignment. Jim Jones knew almost immediately that someone was investigating him; he also knew that neither he nor his power base—the People's Temple—could withstand a critical examination. On Valentine's Day in 1977, Starr was visited by a group of People's Temple lawyers and other personnel. The next day, Starr wrote to Marshall Kilduff:

> A large delegation from the PT called upon me yesterday and convinced me that further publicity at this time would have a bad effect upon the church's ministry. *New West Magazine* has no wish to interfere with the most important work of the PT at this time. *New West Magazine* is very interested in maintaining good community relations. I am therefore asking you not to do the PT story.

A copy of the letter was sent to Jim Jones.

Kilduff then took the story to the *San Francisco Magazine,* but it too turned down the idea after a visit from the same People's Temple delegation. The investigation appeared to be dead until a new ownership took over *New West*. Kevin Starr was out, and Rosalie Muller Wright, the new editor, liked the story and assigned Phil Tracy to work with Marshall Kilduff on the piece.

Jones now attempted to kill the story in two ways. First, he applied pressure on *New West*. Rupert Murdoch, the new owner, was inundated in New York with letters and phone calls, as were the advertisers, who were urged to pull their ads out of the publication. This time most of the letters were not fictitious. They were from the powerful whom Jones had helped. Even the San Francisco branch of the American Civil Liberties Union intervened to try to kill the exposé.

Second, the Temple's propaganda mill went into overtime operation. Reams of heartwarming stories flooded the public and the mailboxes of Temple supporters. Photos of children were used extensively in a series of new brochures about the People's Temple in Guyana. One photograph showed more than fifteen little children holding toys, sucking their thumbs, but all waving "a fond goodbye to Pastor Jones as he leaves to come back to California." In a special Thanksgiving message, Jones wrote:

> Each day the children grow more self-assured, blossoming in all their beauty and creativity, free to express themselves and so healthy and happy . . . The seniors seem to have grown younger . . . the little children look forward eagerly to their visit to the seniors' homes. The medical clinic has been compared to Dr. Schweitzer's hospital in Africa . . .

For the first time, Jones played down the appeal for money as he closed his informative letter with: "I urge you to take advantage of this opportunity to express your gratitude and strengthen your point of contact with the spirit of Love."

When it became apparent that publication of the *New West* article was imminent, Jones panicked, and in what appeared to be a spontaneous decision, hustled the children out of the country to Guyana. The People's Temple Agricultural Project Progress Report for the summer of 1977 was hastily prepared and widely distributed. The brochure depicted a jungle paradise with beautiful children in school situations, playing in the playground, always smiling and waving to the photographer—thus documenting the image that Jones needed to counter the bad publicity expected from the *New West* article.

The Temple's own newspaper, *People's Forum*, cranked out articles about how effectively Jones was helping children, as well as other child-related articles: "Our Children Are Our Wealth," "Black Child Development," "Youth Crime," "Hunger in the U.S.: Children Without Food," and, ironically, "Children Brutalized."

Newspaper rehashes of favorable articles bordered on the ridiculous—for example, the column by Guy Wright in the *San Francisco Examiner*, June 9, 1977. Entitled "Fresh Start in a Jungle for the City Misfits," the piece relied entirely on Jones for information in telling how youngsters were going straight in the jungle under the wise and kind tutelage of Father Jones. Wright ended the article with this alleged statement by a troubled teen-ager of his first day in Jonestown, as Jones described it:

> He [Jones] told about a new arrival who woke up to the tropical dawn, the song of exotic birds, the soft kiss of the trade winds. The young man threw his arms out and shouted, "Man, the Fillmore has seen the last of me!"

To the credit of *New West Magazine*, Jones, with all his power and diverse contacts, failed to control the media in San Francisco totally. Two weeks before publication of its exposé, Jim Jones fled the country, never to return again alive. With him went the remainder of the children and senior citizens. His political workers were transplanted in a foreign country where, without their knowledge, Jones offered their services to the Prime Minister for future elections.

From the jungle, Jones and his faithful planned a counteroffensive. The strategy was threefold: 1) Use the politicians and media to neutralize the *New West* charges of abuse in People's Temple, 2) discredit the informers and obtain glowing comments from "impartial observers," and 3) totally cloud the issue by bringing on Mark Lane, the notorious exposer of government "conspiracies," to act as legal counselor.

Sympathetic politicians and press fell quickly into line. The mayor's office issued the following statement concerning the magazine exposé:

I have read the recent well-publicized article concerning the Reverend Jim Jones and the PT and find it to be a series of allegations with absolutely no hard evidence that the Rev. Jim Jones has violated any laws, either local, state or federal. The Mayor's Office does not and will not conduct any investigations on the Rev. Jones or the PT.

District Attorney Joe Freitas announced, however, that his office, under the jurisdiction of his special prosecutor, Robert Graham, would conduct an investigation into the affairs of People's Temple, but nothing ever came of it.

Columnist Herb Caen wrote that Jones was most anxious to return to the States to defend himself but couldn't act against the advice of his attorney. He then quoted Jones' public relations man, Mike Prokes: "This campaign against Jim is orchestrated at the highest level, perhaps FBI or CIA." Dr. Goodlett leveled his criticism at the people who had given the two reporters their information for the *New West* story, calling them "malcontents, psychoneurotics, and, in some instances, provocateurs—probably Establishment agents."

A notable religious leader, Reverend John V. Moore, former superintendent of the United Methodist Church of northern California, and his wife visited "impressive and amazing" Jonestown during the summer of 1978 to see their two daughters and grandson. On his return, Moore had this to say:

> I had a feeling of freedom. Neither in Georgetown, with twenty-five or thirty people coming and going all the time with total freedom, nor at the project itself did I have any feeling that anybody was being restrained or coerced or intimidated in any way.

The most powerful weapon employed by People's Temple in its counterattack, however, was attorney

Mark Lane, who, after a quick trip to Jonestown, thundered to the press that he would soon file a multimillion-dollar suit against various government agencies for their conspiracy to destroy Jonestown. "The long silence has ended, and the offensive is about to begin," he vowed.

Lane then told the press a story, overlooked in the aftermath of the tragedy, to prove his conspiratorial claim. According to him, twenty employees of Interpol (the International Criminal Police Commission) were sent on a "trans-jungle trek . . . armed with rocket launchers and small arms" to free the children of Jonestown from its reported evil influence. The group, Lane continued,

> was [instructed] to fire on the colony's generator building, darkening the compound, cut their way through barbed wire, and trek over mine fields to rescue the children. . . . Not finding these conditions, they contented themselves with sniping at the compound for six days, and after being invited in and treated well, they felt used by the people who sent them.

Lane also claimed at that time to have a "full statement by the leader" of the alleged battalion, but he never released it.

Goodlett's paper, the *Sun Reporter*, published Lane's findings. Under a picture of happy, smiling Temple children holding a large poster that said, "FREE," the caption read:

> The People's Temple settlement in Jonestown, Guyana, has been described as an armed camp, where people are held against their will and harshly disciplined. Attorney Mark Lane says he has investigated the charges and found them to be false and part of a government-inspired plot to destroy this unique experiment in socialist living. The

youngsters at Jonestown, pictured above, appear to agree with Lane's assessment . . .

In a confidential, attorney/client communication, titled "Projected Offensive Program for the People's Temple," Mark Lane gave Jim Jones the perfect scapegoat(s) he needed to divert attention away from how terrifying life had become in the Temple, especially at Jonestown:

> Even a cursory examination reveals that there has been a coordinated campaign to destroy the People's Temple and to impugn the reputation of its leader, Bishop Jim Jones. This campaign has involved various agencies of the U.S. Government, agencies of various states and the action of numerous individuals who at the present time cannot be proven to have a working relationship with the state or federal authorities. Among the suspect organizations are the Central Intelligence Agency, the Federal Bureau of Investigation, the Internal Revenue Service, the U.S. Post Office, the Federal Communication Commission and their agents and employees.

In the same memo, under the heading "Public Relations Counter-Offensive," Lane suggested that Marceline Jones, Terri Buford, and he "embark upon a campaign following the San Francisco press conference in which we appear on numerous radio and TV talk programs." The aim was to "create an appropriate and trustful image of the People's Temple among organizations on the Left in the U.S. and among Black organizations in the U.S."

At the very end, still another public relations extravaganza was planned—a benefit dinner honoring Jones to show continuing community support for him. Fliers were printed announcing the $25-per-person, tax-deductible dinner program, entitled "A Struggle Against Oppression," at the Hyatt Regency Hotel on December 2, 1978.

Listed as master of ceremonies was the powerful California state assemblyman, Willie L. Brown, Jr. Among the speakers were to be attorneys Mark Lane and Charles Garry, with Dick Gregory the special guest speaker. On the back of the flier, under the endorsements of seventy-six prominent leaders in the Bay Area, was a picture of three beautiful children. Next to the photograph was a quote from Jim Jones:

> When I see the seniors happy and productive—when I see the children of every race gathered together to perform a play—I know we are living to the fullest. Life without principles is devoid of meaning. We have tasted life based on total equality, and now we have no desire to live otherwise.

After the massacre, those invited to speak at the benefit had their excuses. Willie Brown complained that Jones "hustled us politicians," and Dick Gregory blamed the CIA. Mark Lane wrote a book in which he said the "strongest poison" was not that "placed in the mouths of the children in Jonestown," but rather the poison of conspiracy directed at him, Lane, by the government and the press.

> "I walked down a very lonely street.
> There was no one there—just
> Stillness in the lonely street.
> The Wind whistled there.
> I was lost—I know."
>
> David Chaikin, aged fifteen, murdered in
> Jonestown, Guyana

7. The Paralysis and Failure of Government

The carnage at Jonestown resulted from a chain of events—a succession of small tragedies at the heart of which was the lack of basic honesty in government. The children of People's Temple especially were betrayed, as both the federal government and the state of California ignored their rights as human beings and citizens of this country. Most appalling were the actions of the California courts, which willingly served as the tools of People's Temple lawyers. Completely defenseless youngsters and teen-agers were at the mercy of judges who assigned them to lives of living hell. Even after the massacre, those courts and California officials, including Governor Brown, closed ranks in a conspiracy of silence to cover up their own insensitivity in a system that culminated in Jonestown.

Federal investigations and state inquiries have been directed primarily at what money did or did not go into the treasury of People's Temple. No investigation has yet even suggested that the money had an integral relationship to the innocent children. Nor have any studies admitted to the possibility of political corruption, governmental neglect, or the fact that Jones, in large part, short-circuited administrative agencies that could have saved the lives of those children caught up in the madness of his political empire. Instead, congressional inquiries and hearings on Jonestown have found no one to blame.

In preparation for hearings on child abuse in institutions, California Senator Alan Cranston's subcommittee on Child and Human Development raised the issue of foster care children in People's Temple. Senator Cranston asked the General Accounting Office to try to determine whether federal funds had been used to support the Temple's children while they were out of the country. Cranston also wanted to know if any foster care children had died in Jonestown.

In May 1979, in testimony before the committee, Franklin Curtis, associate director of GAO's Human Resources Division, presented little more than demographics on sixteen foster care minors in Jonestown. This typical stance of government to depersonalize human beings served to lessen the impact of their death and make those responsible seem less so. In describing a twelve-year-old black girl who garnered $6,290 in foster-care funds for Jones, the federal government presented the following skeletal profile:

CASE S: This child was in foster care during two time periods with two different, non-related guardians who were People's Temple members. She went to Guyana in August, 1977. Information is not available at this time on who accompanied this child to Guyana. She is on the Department of State's list of verified deceased.

Symbolic of the government's total failure to act on behalf of children for reasons of political expediency, Case S was, in fact, Julie Ann Runnels, a pretty little girl described as "spirited" and "full of life" until the day when she was splattered with chicken blood from one of Jim Jones' "cancer cures." From then on, Julie Ann fought for her independence, her spirit, and finally her life, against insurmountable odds held by every level of government in concert with the powerful cult leader.

Julie Ann's mother, Eddie Jewel Runnels, disabled by blindness, was duped into signing her daughter over to a People's Temple guardianship—one of many that would escape government scrutiny and fatten Jim Jones' treasury. Julie's guardianship file grew thick as People's Temple and authorities responded to pressure from Mrs. Grace Kennedy, the child's great-aunt, who loved the little girl and wanted her to be free and happy. Mrs. Kennedy knew instinctively that things were not right in People's Temple, and she tried to persuade her niece, Eddie Jewel, not to become deeply involved in the church. However, the young mother, who could sign her name only with an "X," was easy prey for Temple lawyers, and soon Julie joined the ranks of other hapless children who were nothing more than bureaucratic paper work for the courts.

Mrs. Kennedy decided to fight. A second job gave her enough money to hire a lawyer. While her resources were no match for the powerful Jones, she did win one small concession—visitation privileges—which created fear and apprehension in People's Temple. Eugene Chaikin and Tim Stoen, who had initially created the guardianship scam, brought in a third attorney, James W. Luther of Ukiah, to handle this particular case. Countering the great-aunt's modest demand for visitation, Luther filed a long brief entitled "Memorandum of Points and Authorities (No. 15408) in the Superior Court of the State of California for the County of Mendocino." This situation was unlike other cases, in which no one looked over their shoulders, and the lawyer wanted the judge to rule out any possibility that Mrs. Kennedy would question them on the grounds that Julie's guardian, Paulette Jackson, was a full-time worker and not a licensed foster care parent:

> Although this is basically a very straightforward case, which clearly justifies the appointment of a guardian by the standards of Section 1440 of the Probate Code, i.e., . . . there has been inserted into this action an irrelevant issue pertaining to custody rights. Mrs. Grace Kennedy, of San Francisco, who has the remote relationship to the minor of "great-aunt," has indicated an intention to contest the appointment of the guardian unless she gets visiting privileges in accordance with a specific schedule that requires overnight visits . . .
>
> What is so unreasonable and surprising about this demand is the fact that a great-aunt has absolutely no custody rights under the law and certainly could not force her wishes upon the mother if the mother did not, because she is in fact blind, require some assistance with the care of her child. The great-aunt seeks to take advantage of the admirable concern of the mother for the highest possible care for her minor by demanding the following:
>
> That, whenever the minor is in San Francisco, she can visit the aunt and that, whenever the minor is in Los Angeles, she can visit another relative. The minor travels with the

mother and the petitioner every weekend to San Francisco and Los Angeles, which means that the minor would be taken away from the normal arrangements of care and training accorded her in order to satisfy this unreasonable demand of her remote relative . . . The mother indicates that in the past she and the child have visited the aunt but have had to terminate the visit because of the great-aunt's disagreements with her on how the child should be raised. The mother is prepared to testify on the stand that the great-aunt has sought to discredit the mother's religious preferences.

Finally, the lawyer begged the court that the wishes of the mother and Jones' appointed guardian "be respected for the growth and well-being of the child and that no remote relative should be permitted to introduce irrelevant issues in a simple guardianship matter."

On November 4, 1974, California Superior Court Judge Arthur B. Broaddus ruled that visitation rights by the great-aunt would not be proper in a guardianship, but he strongly suggested that "the guardian make every effort to see that the great-aunt, Grace Kennedy, has ample and reasonable opportunity to visit the child." He also chided the woman: "The court sees no reason why anyone should discuss religious doctrine before, during, or after any of the visitations." According to Mrs. Kennedy, she was told never to mention the name of Jim Jones around Julie again.

That was a difficult point of the court order for the great-aunt to obey. When Julie came for her occasional visits, she was always depressed when it was time to return to the Temple. She told her aunt, "I want to come and stay with you and go to the school across the street." On one occasion, she appeared in dirty rags and wearing soleless shoes. Mrs. Kennedy took her to Sears and outfitted her with shoes, socks, underwear, and a coat. She bought her an Easter basket once, but, as with other things, Julie Ann was afraid to take it back. The aunt said that when the child would return from a visit to her, "the People's Temple people would pick her soul and beat her if she told me anything." When Julie was still only seven years old, Grace Kennedy recalled dropping her off at the Temple: "I'll never forget the look on Julie Ann's face. She was transformed into a different person as fear spread across her little face."

Mrs. Kennedy did whatever she could to protect her great-niece from Jim Jones. After the child began to take the long weekend bus trips to Los Angeles to insure a packed church for Jones, her aunt attempted to make arrangements for Julie's father to visit her. But when the great-aunt or the father entered the Los Angeles Temple church, they were insulted and searched but never got to see Julie Ann. Finally, the little girl stopped coming to see her relative. She dropped out of sight, and the caring great-aunt never saw her again alive.

Little Julie Ann Runnels and the other children were swept up by events they were unable to understand. Like sticks in a stream, they were carried away to the distant land of Guyana. They could have been saved more than once if only the authorities—local, state, federal—had not been compromised and subsequently become unable or unwilling to act on behalf of the children.

On March 31, 1977, the American Embassy in Georgetown was informed by the Guyanese Minister of Foreign Affairs that 380 "immigrants" from People's Temple would be arriving in Guyana. Jones told Guyanese officials that these immigrants "represent[ed] some of the most skilled and progressive elements of [his] organization and, as such, [were] most vulnerable to state repression on the part of American authorities." In August 1977, the first group arrived, accompanied by a $500,000 check to "assist in the settlement of these skilled people"—who were, as it turned out, young children (including Julie Ann) and senior citizens.

Both American and Guyanese officials, who were expecting hearty adult pioneers, were alarmed to see so many young children flooding into Georgetown and quickly disappearing into the agricultural settlement in the northern jungle. Their concern heightened when it was pointed out to them by Joe Mazor, a private investigator from San Francisco, that the children were being held there against their will. Mazor claimed he had been retained by the parents of seven People's Temple children to arrange for their return to the United States. Consul Richard McCoy's official posture was reflected in his correspondence with the State department:

> Since a custody dispute is not at issue, consul suggests that if parents can afford trip, they should consider coming to Guyana and, with the help of Mazor's local attorney, pick up the children and return with them to the U.S.

Jones sensed the growing concern and started a public relations campaign that labeled many of the children "troubled youths" whom the courts had entrusted to his care because of People's Temple's proven success with such delinquents. Still, lower-echelon Guyanese immigration officials expressed worry about the number of children entering the country without parents, but were told by their superiors that their anxieties were ill-founded.

American authorities also noted that there were many more children at Jonestown than was normal for the few families and parents there at that time. On August 30, 1977, Richard McCoy confronted Jones and asked him point-blank if the children were in Guyana illegally. Jones was visibly surprised by the question, but evenly answered that the children were court-appointed to People's Temple custody. However, McCoy returned to Georgetown and immediately cabled the State Department in Washington the following message concerning the legality of approximately 130 to 150 American young people then residing in Jonestown under questionable status:

> . . . FRANKLY, ENTIRE SITUATION SEEMS VERY STRANGE SINCE CHILDREN FOR MOST PART HAVE ONLY BEEN IN GUYANA NO MORE THAN FOUR MONTHS. SOMEONE HAD TO APPLY FOR PASSPORTS FOR THEM AND ALLOW THEM TO TRAVEL. A SEPARATE QUESTION PERTAINS TO THE CHILDREN WHO HAVE BEEN AWARDED TO JONES AND OTHER MEMBERS OF THE PEOPLE'S TEMPLE BY THE STATE OF CALIFORNIA. PRESUMABLY COURTS THERE AGREED TO THEIR REMOVAL FROM STATE JURISDICTION WHEN THEY WERE BROUGHT HERE. IF NOT, ARE THEN JONES AND PEOPLE'S TEMPLE IN VIOLATION OF CALIFORNIA LAW? ACTION REQUESTED: SINCE ABOUT 130–150 CHILDREN ARE HERE WHO REPORTEDLY WERE FORMERLY CONSIDERED TO BE WARDS OF THE STATE OF CALIFORNIA, REQUEST DEPARTMENT CONTACT APPROPRIATE STATE OFFICIAL CONCERNING THIS QUESTION AND INFORM EMBASSY WHETHER THIS WILL BE AN ADDITIONAL PROBLEM . . .

Upon receipt of this cable, the State Department telephoned California officials. On September 13, 1977, the following message was drafted and sent to McCoy in Guyana:

> DEPT. OFFICER CONTACTED CALIFORNIA STATE DEPT. OF BENEFITS PAYMENTS, COUNSEL FOR CHILD SUPPORT AND SUPPORT ENFORCEMENT DIVISION FOR RESPONSE TO EMBASSY'S QUESTION . . . STATE OFFICIAL STATED THAT COUNTY OFFICIALS HAVE PRIMARY RESPONSIBILITY IN

CUSTODY MATTERS. STATE OFFICIAL UNABLE TO ASSIST WITHOUT NAMES OF CHILDREN AND CALIFORNIA PLACE OF RESIDENCE. AT PRESENT HE HAD NO KNOWLEDGE OF GENERALIZED OR SPECIFIC COMPLAINTS ABOUT CHILDREN ALLEGEDLY REMOVED FROM CALIFORNIA. STATE OFFICIAL CONFIRMS THAT COURT PERMISSION IS REQUIRED TO REMOVE WARDS OF THE COURT.

Even though California officials responded to the State Department, confirming it was illegal for children to be removed from the United States without court orders, and requested the names of the children in question, the American Embassy in Guyana never pursued the matter aggressively. After several futile attempts to obtain the 150 names from Jones, the matter was dropped. It remained a low priority even after the massacre. In a 782-page report of the main investigation by the House Foreign Affairs Committee (*The Assassination of Representative Leo J. Ryan and the Jonestown, Guyana, Tragedy*), only two paragraphs were devoted to the children. One of those paragraphs, however, stated:

> The Staff Investigative Group [of the committee] was informed by State Department witnesses that the U.S. Embassy in Guyana was never asked by California welfare officials to check on the welfare and whereabouts of California foster children reportedly living in Jonestown. The U.S. Embassy, however, was aware that some foster children may have been living there and asked the State Department to determine whether it was legal for such wards of the state to leave the United States. One department witness said that he queried appropriate California authorities and was told that court permission was required to take them out of the state. This same official also discerned some reluctance on the part of these authorities to talk about the subject.

It is safe to say that the "reluctance" which the State Department encountered on the subject of children being spirited out of the country during the summer of 1977 is now standard policy throughout every branch and level of state government in California. No one with any authority will discuss the subject of how or why the bureaucracy failed to save the lives of 276 minors.

First, as the President of the United States sets the tone for key decision making in the federal government, so, too, does a governor set the tone in state government. While Governor Brown respectfully attended the funeral of Representative Ryan, he, like all the other politicians, has said nothing about his or the state's role in the removal of children to Jonestown. Appearing on a morning TV talk show, *Donahue,* before announcing his candidacy for President of the United States, Brown was confronted by Mrs. Marilyn Wood, a first-year law student living in Chicago. The dialogue, as taken from *Donahue* transcript No. 10089, October 8, 1979, went as follows:

> AUDIENCE: [Marilyn Wood] The governor mentioned that he was concerned about the poor and millions of starving children. I wondered why he wasn't more concerned about the guardianships of the hundreds of children he signed over to Reverend Jim Jones.
>
> GOV. BROWN: That's not true.
>
> AUDIENCE: There was an article*—
>
> GOV. BROWN: I know there was an article, but that article was false. The state of California provides money, as well as the federal government, for local welfare programs, aid to dependent children, as well as foster care, and those programs are supervised at the local county level. And our Department of Social Welfare has inves-

---

* A seven-part series by this writer for the *Chicago Sun-Times* (June 1979), in which the author charged California officials with a cover-up, since they refused to talk to a federal Investigation Unit about the children of Jonestown. Attempts to reach even Gov. Brown's press secretaries for rebuttal at that time were futile.

tigated those problems and has required the counties and local governments to tighten up. But that was never done within the approval of the state government. In fact, it was done by misrepresentation at the local level and was never brought to our attention.

AUDIENCE: But they have quotes and pictures of you with Jones, commenting on how great he was, and what a responsible person he was—

GOV. BROWN: That is not true. The whole—and this is why I think it's a good idea that you raised that. I went to a church once on the Martin Luther King Memorial, and it was supported by the whole black community of San Francisco. That particular church happened to be Jim Jones' church. That's the one they picked. I went to the pulpit. I spoke for three or four minutes and I walked out of there. That's the only time I had any contact with that particular organization. And I said nothing in praise of Mr. Jones because I had never met him before. I spoke about Martin Luther King and the importance of his example for the country.

AUDIENCE: Are you denying, then, this article, this series of articles?

GOV. BROWN: Yes, it's totally false.

AUDIENCE: You had no involvement. You're not involved in any kind of a cover-up—and the California state government is not involved in any kind of a cover-up involving these children.

GOV. BROWN: That's right, and if you have any information to the contrary, I'd like to hear about it. I'd be very interested.

AUDIENCE: I think you should read this series of articles. It was very important.

GOV. BROWN: Well, I've read more things about me that I don't either believe or agree with, that that wouldn't surprise me. But if you have them, I wish you would send them to me and I'll try to straighten the person out.

Mrs. Wood sent the articles to the Governor, but never once did he or his staff contact the *Sun-Times* or the writer. This silence was consistent with the Governor's silence to Gordon Lindsay, a freelance investigative reporter, who repeatedly warned Jerry Brown of the cruelty and misuse of public funds in People's Temple. It was the same silence experienced by former Temple members who were brave enough to walk away from the reign of terror and who informed the Governor's office in Sacramento of Jim Jones' crimes. Governor Brown, like other politicians up and down the line, had wittingly or unwittingly been compromised by Jones. He had accepted People's Temple contributions and the help of the church's children in his electoral campaign. He had known, too, the potential votes Jones' "troops" commanded for future campaigns for higher office.

Unfortunately, even in light of the Jonestown mass murders, Jerry Brown continued to disregard the basic rights of children in his state. Six days before his appearance on the *Donahue* show, he failed to sign Bill SB444, which called for "tightened standards for residential group homes for more than 6,000 children." This bill, which would have "barred the hiring of convicted sex offenders" and "required license renewal annually rather than every other year," was not acted upon even after staff personnel in both the state's private and public institutions were arrested for raping and sexually molesting children.

Immediately following the tragic events in Jonestown, James Polk of *NBC News* did a piece on Vincent Lopez, a foster child who was in Guyana without his parents. Polk raised the possibility that there might have been more foster children who had perished with the Lopez boy. When bureaucrats in the California Legislature and county welfare offices speculated that as many as 150 to

200 People's Temple children were wards of the state, Senator Alan Cranston, as mentioned previously, asked the General Accounting Office to investigate the matter.

Beginning in December 1978, GAO searched mountains of readouts from California welfare computers, then reported that thirty-one foster children were known to have been placed under People's Temple guardianships while in the United States. Later, they estimated that sixteen foster children were sent to Guyana.* The GAO acknowledged that "their estimates of children in guardianships were based on figures California officials [were] feeding [them]." Most important, their study involved only 13 of more than 100 counties in California, a significant point, since Mendocino County Welfare Officer Dennis Denny, who fought Jones on his poor foster care program, stated: "Jones filed the guardianships in counties all over California to avoid suspicion." California judges who ruled on the guardianships also joined in the conspiracy of silence by never responding to questions on guardianships raised by GAO's congressional inquiry.

The investigation Governor Brown referred to on the *Donahue* show was conducted by his own political appointments: the Department of Health and Welfare head, Mario Obledgo, and Marion J. Woods, director of the Department of Social Services. In a total whitewash of the guardianship scandal, both men removed their agencies from any blame in the deaths of the children. At a joint press conference, Mario Obledgo acknowledged that he "agonized over the whole situation," but added, "I doubt anything could have been done to prevent

---

* With extremely limited resources and no subpoena power, the *Chicago Sun-Times* investigation found evidence that fifty-six People's Temple children were processed through the guardianship courts, thirty-five of whom are known to have perished in Guyana on November 18, 1978.

transportation of children to Guyana by their natural parents and legal guardians." He and Marion Woods lamely called for "bold legislative action to consolidate welfare agencies which allow some children to fall through the cracks." An example of this is one young girl from People's Temple who was under foster care and guardianship and was taken to Guyana. The GAO investigation listed her as deceased; California said she was alive and attending school in California. No one cared enough to resolve the discrepancy. The report of Obledgo and Woods concluded: ". . . our investigation disclosed no children were in Guyana who were under the supervision and care of the state's Department of Social Services at the time of the Guyana incident." With that statement, California political appointees exonerated themselves, their departments, and their state government. Governor Brown, ever with an eye on the Presidency, could inform the American public that no one was at fault for the untimely deaths of close to 300 children because they had been with their "parents and legal guardians."

Nevertheless, the GAO investigation uncovered evidence that San Francisco County officials closed the case files of children under their jurisdiction because they "didn't know their wards had left the country" and/or had "lost contact with the foster care family." GAO also told Senator Cranston about the "Assignment-of-Custody" documents, by which natural parents and legal guardians in People's Temple were convinced or coerced to sign over, to three members of Jones' hierarchy, unlimited authority and control over their children. These three custodians were stationed—one in San Francisco, one in Georgetown, Guyana, and another in Jonestown—at checkpoints along the route the children took to their final destination. All this activity was totally ignored by California officials, with the exception of one man who tried to make his voice heard in the bureaucratic wilderness.

J. C. Ortiz was a State Health and Welfare Department investigator under the jurisdiction of Mario Obledgo before his job in that state agency was "reorganized" out of existence. Ortiz became aware of People's Temple thirteen months before the massacre, when Dennis Denny, director of the Mendocino County Department of Social Services, filed a complaint, alleging that children under court-ordered guardianships were being shipped out of the country to Guyana and were being subjected to mental and physical abuse in Jonestown. Denny complained that he "didn't know who to trust in [his] department because of previous mass infiltration" by such People's Temple members as Linda Amos, Marceline Jones, Jim Randolph, Joyce Shaw, Grace Stoen, and Larry Layton.

Ortiz immediately obtained from Mendocino County the names of all children under guardianships and legal adoptions, as well as those of children and adolescents from other county probation departments. He decided to begin his investigation by interviewing People's Temple members who were legal guardians or who had been given responsibility for children by public agencies. His first interview was with George Donald Beck, who refused to tell Ortiz anything and referred him to Temple lawyer Charles Garry. That prompted the investigator to draft the following memo to his department's legal division.

> A recent investigation into the activities of a religious organization revealed that person(s) may have been seduced by false promises and/or misrepresentation for the purpose of taking such person(s) out of the continental United States, a violation of California Penal Code 207.

Furthermore, ex-members of this religious group have alleged that the person(s) abducted are not allowed to return to the continental United States and that such person(s) are being held for involuntary servitude, a violation of California Penal Code 181.

Please advise if there are any federal or state statutes which would require a parent or guardian to reveal the whereabouts of their children under guardianship, children under adoption or children under the care of their natural parents.

Please call me if you require further information.

On December 23, 1977, a legal division lawyer, Rhoda Haberman, advised Ortiz that there was no provision of law that "would require a parent or guardian to produce their children or minor wards without some provable allegations of neglect, abandonment, or abuse." However, Haberman did allow that any court that ordered a guardianship was responsible and that no child under such jurisdiction could leave the state "without the express permission of that court [Probate Code Section 1500]."

Mendocino authorities told Ortiz that "there was supposed to be a yearly follow-up on all placements where welfare funds were involved." However, People's Temple shrewdly had children from one county placed in another, switched the minors among themselves, and moved frequently, making it almost impossible to check on the children's whereabouts. Prior to 1977, there were no statutes in California requiring any form of investigation into the backgrounds of people applying for guardianships. When the statute was changed, it still didn't affect most of the children in People's Temple, because they had already been placed and removed from the country.

Frustrated over the lack of legal and governmental

protection for children who were being shipped out of the United States, Ortiz went to Janet Kespohl, a deputy sheriff in Mendocino County, to see if he could coordinate his own investigation with anything the sheriff's office was conducting against People's Temple. Deputy Kespohl informed him that there wasn't an open inquiry on the guardianship issue but that the case had been raised with the attorney general. She suggested he contact Deputy Attorney General W. Eric Collins. Said Ortiz:

> I made numerous calls to the San Francisco A.G.'s office in order to establish a liaison between that office and ours so that we could have a coordinated investigative effort. For the longest period, my calls were not returned. The message I left was that I was an investigator with the Department of Health and wanted to talk to someone regarding the People's Temple. If my memory serves me right, I believe I received one call when I was out of town. Later, I did manage to contact someone affiliated with that office who informed me that their office had not initiated any investigations regarding the People's Temple. As of this date, I do not know or have knowledge of any investigation initiated by the attorney general's office in or out of the San Francisco office.

Postal inspectors were very helpful to Ortiz. They revealed that Social Security checks, both gold and green, were being sent to Guyana via one of three post office boxes that Jones had in a San Francisco post office. Although this practice was stopped by an HEW directive, postal officials felt that the checks were still being sent to Guyana in unidentifiable manila envelopes, which, by law, they were not permitted to open.

Ortiz hit a stone wall with the U.S. Immigration Service. "In essence," he said, "what Immigration was conveying to me was that they did not have any information which could help me identify those children who were now in Guyana." He then visited the Alameda County Probation Department because Mendocino County had given him a list of children and adolescents who had been placed in People's Temple by that department. There, too, Ortiz was stonewalled. The department (which was also infiltrated by People's Temple) informed him that the records were sealed and unavailable to other agencies because juvenile records were confidential.

The most impenetrable department, not only for Ortiz but also for the U.S. State Department, was the California State Department of Benefit Payments. Even after the investigator supplied that agency with the names of the children under guardianships or probations, it never notified the courts that had ultimate jurisdiction over the minors. Lieutenant Governor Mervyn Dymally, who was totally devoted to Jim Jones, had appointed Mari Goldman to the department; she has denied directing crucial persons to answer no inquiries, questions, or investigations involving People's Temple. These were the same people whom the House Foreign Affairs Committee termed "reluctant to talk about the children of Jonestown" after the massacre.

Ortiz felt by now that almost all of the children had been taken to Guyana, so he decided to look into the group homes owned and operated by People's Temple. On November 30, 1977, he visited Happy Acres, which kicked back most of its state and federal payments to Jim Jones. There, he found irregularities in the MediCal benefits and submitted a complaint to the MediCal Fraud Unit in San Francisco. Nothing came of it.

Ortiz then contacted the Touchettes' Family Care Home and discovered that all the residents "had obtained Social Security numbers in numerical order."

Although the Social Security office thought this was very strange, it never bothered to investigate. Ortiz called his inquiry "without a doubt the most frustrating case that I have ever encountered. It appeared that the very agencies that could have helped me either were restricted from giving me information or just did not want to get involved." He ended with the following conclusions:

> Jim Jones had a very sophisticated organization. He had infiltrated the system long before the investigation by our department ensued. Jones had members in Facility Licensing, the Mendocino Welfare Department, and the Juvenile Probation Department. He evidently had influence with various county district attorney offices, and with various other elected officials.
>
> There are indications that the People's Temple penetrated the government at the city, county, and state levels.
>
> The investigation also revealed that children/adolescents were being placed by both the courts and the probation department with no follow-up. Mendocino County, along with other counties in question, could not account for the whereabouts of those clients under their jurisdiction.
>
> My first setback was the legal opinion of our legal office, which informed me that there was "no provision of law that would require a parent or guardian to produce their children or minor wards without some provable allegations of neglect." I could not believe that a person did not have to make accountable the whereabouts of his children when asked by an investigating officer.
>
> I do not feel that any one agency is responsible for the circumstances which brought on Jonestown. I do feel that the tragedy might have been prevented if a combined effort by all agencies (federal, state, and local) had been initiated.

On June 6, 1978, J. C. Ortiz submitted his report on People's Temple to higher officials within the Health Department. The report, which at first gathered dust, became, after the massacre, a hot item in California political circles as bureaucrats tried to prevent its publication, at the same time minimizing its importance. The Ortiz report was known to Senator Cranston during his subcommittee hearing in Los Angeles, and, subsequently, the head of the California Department of Social Services was invited to testify. On May 31, 1979, Department Deputy Phil Manriquez, representing Director Marion Woods, went before the Senate inquiry panel. Following is some dialogue between Senator Cranston and Mr. Manriquez:

SEN. CRANSTON: Going on to another matter, the GAO has provided me with documents from state files indicating that the state of California had received complaints about the involvement of the People's Temple in foster care placements and the possible conflict of interest in the employment of Marceline Jones—Reverend Jim Jones' wife—in the Department of Health's licensing and certification unit as early as July of 1977. These documents indicate that the state investigation terminated—despite allegations of all sorts of abuses in the summer of 1978. Why was that investigation terminated?

MR. MANRIQUEZ: Senator, I'm unable to answer that question. At that time, the responsibility for all of these programs before was in a department that was called the Department of Health. We inherited their records. As a result of a reorganization, this department then became responsible for the social service programs, July of last year. . . .

SEN. CRANSTON: Well, have you made an effort to find out why it was terminated?

MR. MANRIQUEZ: Yes, we have. . . . I have talked to the investigator (Ortiz) and he assures me that he had information that there were several federal agencies that were carrying on investigations about the People's

Temple allegations, and that he recommended that the state adopt a role of supporting those investigations, rather than carrying on with the investigation that he had going on at that time.

SEN. CRANSTON: What federal investigations?

MR. MANRIQUEZ: He mentioned investigations being carried out by the U.S. postal authorities.

SEN. CRANSTON: What would they be investigating?

MR. MANRIQUEZ: It's my understanding that there had been allegations made about public assistance warrants being "laundered" through various collection points in the state, and that there was a strong possibility that there was a misuse of U.S. mails involved.

SEN. CRANSTON: Did the state contact the federal authorities and offer to help them?

MR. MANRIQUEZ: I don't know, Senator.

SEN. CRANSTON: I've looked at the report, and in view of the shocking nature of the allegations, it's rather incredible that the state's investigation would be dropped without any certainty as to what would be carried on in regard to the report.

MR. MANRIQUEZ: Yes, we felt the same way; and when we saw it, we saw all of the open ends in that investigation; and that's what prompted our department, then, to take on some investigative activities. However, we did not have responsibility for the program until after July. By the time we got started in our investigation, we had the Guyana incident occur in November; and then, of course, the emphasis of our investigation then shifted over to that of the People's Temple.

SEN. CRANSTON: Do you think anything more could be done to find out why that investigation was dropped? (No response) I'd like to urge you to think that over and . . . see if you can't find out more on that. Because it's very strange, in view of the allegations. And I wouldn't think that just assuming the Post Office Department was going to look into abuse of the mails would be a very effective way of getting at the bottom of the sort of circumstances that were going on there. And had an investigation continued, things that occurred thereafter might not have occurred.

MR. MANRIQUEZ: I can't answer that, Senator.

SEN. CRANSTON: Well, you can look into . . . that and try to find out more about what happened to that investigation.

MR. MANRIQUEZ: Yes.

SEN. CRANSTON: The GAO report indicates that six of the foster children went to Guyana after October of 1977—when the investigation began—and three of the six went after June of 1978—when the investigation terminated. The report that was released earlier this month by the House Committee investigating the death of Representative Ryan states:

> State Department witnesses said that the U.S. Embassy in Guyana was never asked by California welfare officials to check on the welfare and whereabouts of California foster children reportedly living in Jonestown. The U.S. Embassy, however, was aware that some foster children may have been living there and asked the Department of State to determine whether it was legal for such wards of the state to leave the United States. One department witness stated that he queried appropriate California authorities and was told that court permission was required to take them out of the state.

Do you have any comment on that?

MR. MANRIQUEZ: Yes, Senator. First of all, I believe that we have to realize that in terms of our department and the involvement of the Aid to Families with Dependent Children foster-care component, we are talking about only a segment of the overall foster care area. Foster care that might involve legal guardianship and does not involve an AFDC-BHI [Aid to Families with Dependent Children-Boarding Homes Income] payment would not come under the purview of our responsibility or our ability to investigate.

The GAO has reported that there was only one child in Guyana that was an active AFDC-BHI case, thereby becoming our responsibility. If there were six children in foster care in Guyana, they would have been six of that thirty-seven, that group of thirty-seven children that were under a legal guardianship type of arrangement, and, thus, would not be within our area of investigation.

As was indicated in this report, there were nineteen children that at one point in time had received payments under the AFDC-BHI program. Eighteen of those had been discontinued prior to their arrival in Guyana. They had been returned to their parents, in most cases, were adopted, or had been placed under some type of a legal guardianship arrangement, which then took them out of the sphere of our responsibility.

The Ortiz report is devastating to the state of California's credibility for investigating itself. It is obvious that a number of state officials knew about the dark side of Jim Jones but remained silent. However, many were reportedly relieved when Jones left the country in 1977. The very government that the cult leader viewed with growing suspicion and fear as he became more dependent on drugs and increasingly paranoiac was his confederate in sealing the fate of his entrapped followers.

Ortiz was especially critical of the state attorney general's office. Many instances showed that the law enforcement agency was safely in Jim Jones' pocket. Jones told his followers more than once, "I met with Younger [Evelle J. Younger, former state attorney general] and he is on our side." And to others, he said, "Don't think you can go to the attorney general . . . We have friends everywhere." Those who wrote letters, made phone calls, and personally visited Younger's office to make complaints against Jones quickly learned his claims were not exaggerated.

A Ukiah Baptist minister, Richard G. Taylor, became alarmed over the techniques of Jim Jones. His concern started with the flood of cakes and cards sent to the ill and the troubled, the "overkill" selling of Jones' wondrous faith healings. Taylor's misgivings increased as tales of beatings and abuse in People's Temple reached his attention, culminating in an incident involving a woman he knew, Mrs. Maxine Harp. After Mrs. Harp's mysterious death (designated officially "suicide by hanging"—yet the body was found lying on a chest in her garage), her home was ransacked, then locked up by People's Temple. When only a very superficial local investigation took place, Taylor wrote a long letter to the state attorney general's office, urging an investigation of both Mrs. Harp's death and Jim Jones.

In response to his letter, Taylor received a call from a deputy in the attorney general's office, asking the minister to visit him. When Taylor showed up for the appointment armed with other evidence, the deputy informed him that there could be no investigation because there was "insufficient evidence." Immediately thereafter, Taylor's wife started getting threatening calls from sources who the Taylors felt certain "originated from the People's Temple."

Another example involved contractor J. R. Purifoy, who had documentation that proved People's Temple was illegally transferring real estate. "If people wouldn't sign over their deeds, he [Jones] would have them notarized in advance." Purifoy called the attorney general's office in Sacramento with this information. The same day, Jones called Purifoy to say that "the A.G. notified [him] of the call." Purifoy made a tape recording of this phone conversation, in which Jones confirmed he had major contacts in that office: "If it hadn't been for my connections in the A.G.'s office," Jones told the planning commission, "they would have come swarming down all over us."

As mentioned before, San Francisco Mayor George Moscone publicly declined to investigate People's Temple after the *New West* article appeared in August 1977, claiming it had broken no laws. His district attorney, Joe Freitas, conducted a mild investigation and also found that no laws had been broken. He did concede that some of the People's Temple activities were "at least unsavory and raised substantial moral and noncriminal legal questions." Later, Freitas, who was fond of his former assistant, Tim Stoen, tried to help in Stoen's custody battle for his son. The district attorney wrote Representative Phil Burton and asked him to urge the American Ambassador, John Burke, to attend the custody court procedures in Georgetown, Guyana, to guarantee that "due process was being observed." Shortly thereafter, however, Marceline Jones visited the Congressman and asked him not to become involved. Apparently, Mrs. Jones was more convincing than Joe Freitas, for the Ambassador was never notified of the legal hearings and therefore did not attend.

Steven Katsaris had exhausted his political friends and personal resources in his desperate attempts to get help for himself and other Concerned Relatives from the bureaucracy. The one person he had been unable to contact was Mayor Moscone. On a flight to Washington one day to lobby for the Concerned Relatives, Katsaris found George Moscone and his press secretary, Milt Wax, sitting across the aisle from him. During the long flight, Katsaris poured out his anguish over his daughter, Maria, whom Jones had brainwashed and was sexually abusing. Moscone ended the conversation by saying,

"Gee, Steve, I'm sorry to hear all of this. I'll say a lot of prayers for Maria."

Many of the survivors of People's Temple were bitter toward the President and Mrs. Carter as well. After Jim Jones' highly publicized meeting with Mrs. Carter and his public endorsement of her husband, a number of ex-members wrote the First Lady. Mickey Touchette remembered:

> We told her what he was doing and what was involved and what kind of a man he was, and she turned a deaf ear to us. . . . All the politicians knew, the whole bureaucratic structure of the country knew about Jim Jones, and they, too, turned a deaf ear to us.

Guyanese officials contend that even those among them who had great doubts about Jones let him "slide through" because higher-ups in that country felt Jones "had great clout in the White House."

For an administration that has so loudly espoused the cause of human rights around the world, the record of the Carter government in the Jonestown affair raises serious questions about the nature of this commitment. In the spring of 1977, Carter made a "major" speech to the UN on human rights; he then appointed Patricia Derian, an early supporter of his election campaign, to head the State Department's Office of Human Rights and Humanitarian Affairs, with the mission of checking into repression and torture around the world.

Unfortunately for the children of Jonestown, the role of the State Department and our Embassy in Guyana was one of bumbling, neglect, incompetence, and deceit. The repeated pleas of parents concerning their children held at Jonestown, and the requests of other government agencies for information, were met with indifference. The Department never acknowledged the receipt of the April

11, 1978, statement by the Concerned Relatives accusing Jones of human rights violations (see Appendix), and it is unlikely that people on the level of Derian or Secretary of State Vance ever saw the document before the massacre.

Nevertheless, it is clear that at the level of the Embassy in Guyana and at higher levels of the State Department in Washington, there was considerable awareness of the problem. In replying to a request to Vance from Sherwin Harris of Lafayette, California, that the Department bring pressure on the government of Guyana to make Jones halt his abuses against Harris' daughter Liane and others at Jonestown, Hodding Carter III, State Department spokesman, wrote on June 16, 1978:

> As part of the traditional and internationally sanctioned protection services, officers of the American Embassy in Georgetown, Guyana, periodically visit the People's Agricultural Temple located at Jonestown, Guyana. These officers have been free to move about the grounds and speak privately to any individuals, including persons who were believed by their family and friends to be held there against their will. It is the opinion of these officers, reinforced by conversations with local officials who deal with the People's Temple, that it is improbable anyone is being held in bondage. In general, the people appear healthy, adequately fed and housed, and satisfied with their lives on what is a large farm. Many do hard, physical labor, but there is no evidence of persons being forced to work beyond their capacity or against their will.

The letter further suggested that if Harris wanted information about a specific individual, he should send the person's name, and date and place of birth, to the Department's Office of Special Services, and during the next visit to Jonestown an Embassy officer would seek to speak privately to the individual and report back. This was in reply to Harris' letter in which he mentioned his daughter Liane several times.

In fact, in the six months previous to November 18, 1978, there was no visit to Jonestown by an Embassy officer. On June 27, 1978, a couple from Ohio had written the Embassy about their concern for the safety of their daughter and three grandchildren in the Guyana jungle. On the morning of November 18, 1978, a few hours before their daughter and grandchildren would die of cyanide poisoning, Wayne and Betty Study received a response to their letter from Douglas V. Ellice, Jr.:

> My predecessor, Mr. Richard McCoy, was unable to visit the People's Temple Agricultural Community on August 1, 1978 because the nearest airstrip had been closed by heavy rainfall. He has since assumed a new position elsewhere and I have been assigned to Georgetown as his successor.
>
> I visited the Community yesterday and spoke to Bonnie. She asked me to relay to you her assurance that she is well and happy. . . .

On two occasions, the Social Security Administration, prompted by negative media reports on People's Temple, wrote the American Embassy in Guyana, requesting verification that Temple members were "being coerced" into giving their Social Security checks to the church against their will. To the first inquiry, the Embassy responded that the recipients were receiving their checks and "were making no assignments of their right to future SSA monthly payments." The second inquiry, inspired by Deborah Blakey's allegations that "the Temple received over $65,000 in SS checks per month . . . and only a fraction of the income of senior citizens in the care of the Temple was being used for their benefit," was dated October 13, 1978, and asked the Embassy again to investigate. This request was never answered, but after the tragedy, the press reported that hundreds of checks had been found in Jim Jones' house.

In direct violation of the Federal Communications Commission regulations, Jones communicated in code between Jonestown and the San Francisco church. With these coded messages, he controlled the transfer of children and, later, adults of People's Temple into his jungle concentration camp. His medical staff also used this system to order illegal drugs, guns, and ammunition for the Guyana settlement. After many complaints from ham radio operators (including Al and Jeannie Mills of Concerned Relatives, who tried monitoring them but were unable to), the FCC started to tape the broadcasts. Many violations were recorded in the critical time-frame between May and September, 1977, the period during which large numbers of children were taken on "vacations."

In November 1977, the San Francisco office of the FCC sent an active file of People's Temple violations for transmitting false and deceptive call-signs to Washington headquarters with the recommendation that "the operator's license be revoked." However, not only did someone in Washington decide there weren't "sufficient grounds" to revoke the license, he warned the People's Temple. Jones responded with a flood of letters to the White House and Congress claiming "harassment." Violation notices were still being sent by the FCC to People's Temple as late as October 30, 1978, but Jones' operation continued to "transmit in code and use a frequency out of an amateur band."

In June 1978, Senator Hayakawa's office in San Francisco received a letter from Mrs. Clara Bouquet that included serious charges that children and old people were being forced to endure inhuman conditions in Jonestown, and a plea for the Senator's help. Mr. Hayakawa sent her letter to the FBI for their attention. They subsequently interviewed Mrs. Bouquet, whose son would soon be murdered, but "found no basis for further action." The FBI did suggest to Senator Hayakawa, however, that he bring the matter to the attention of the State Department.

One by one, every governmental checkpoint designed to stem corruption, infractions, and nonrepresentation failed or was compromised at a time when it was of paramount importance that action be taken in order to save lives and prevent human abuses. That failure insured the subsequent anarchy and the terrible fate awaiting hundreds of vulnerable children who had been betrayed.

In the last moments, Julie Ann Runnels fought desperately for life. It took two strong adults to extinguish the spirit that her great-aunt and others had so admired. Betrayed by the American political system, Julie died along with her many companions. When she heard the news about the mass deaths in Jonestown, Grace Kennedy was heartbroken. In anger and grief, she pounded on the door of People's Temple Church, shouting for Julie's blind mother to come outside. Eventually, Eddie Jewel confronted the great-aunt. Still brainwashed, she insisted Julie wasn't really dead. "Jim Jones will see to it," she said, returning to her mysterious world inside the Temple.

Soon afterward, the Runnels child was listed with the verified dead; and because of her death, Grace Kennedy obtained what the courts of California and Jim Jones had denied her when the child was alive. Julie Ann was cremated after her mother signed her body over to Grace Kennedy. The child's remains are with the one person who truly cared, in a home filled with a little girl's new clothes, an Easter basket, and mixed memories of what could have been.

> "You have to put fear aside and do what you think is right."
>
> Leo Ryan, on the eve of his trip to Jonestown

8. The Quest of Leo Ryan

Representative Leo Ryan was the first United States Congressman ever to have been killed in the line of duty. A loner in Congress who deeply believed that government should be responsive to the people it serves, Ryan sought his own answers to things that bothered him and his constituents. He was known on The Hill for his investigative ventures, such as living with a black family in Watts, California, after the 1965 riots, spending a week in Folsom Prison as an inmate to learn about prison life, and traveling to Newfoundland to document the killing of baby seals. Called a "headline grabber" by cynics, Ryan was regarded by those close to him as an impassioned and determined advocate for human rights and social justice. In the words of his legislative assistant, Jackie

Speier, "He was tough as nails and at every point in time, his own man. He could never be counted on for his vote by any group—and thus paid a heavy price for his independence in the House."

Ryan was born in Lincoln, Nebraska, on May 5, 1925, to Irish parents who were both crusading journalists. After serving in the Navy during World War II, he completed undergraduate and postgraduate work in Elizabethan drama at The Creighton University. He taught high school English first in Nebraska, then in California, where he entered local politics as a reformer and became a member of the State Legislature in 1962. Elected to Congress in 1972, he went to Washington convinced he could make a real difference there. Twice married and divorced and the father of five, Ryan delighted in taking the time to guide schoolchildren from his district around the Capitol and in turning his office into a classroom. Late on Friday afternoons, he would sit in his old-fashioned barber's chair and discuss "people problems" with his staff. After reviewing such concerns, he would relax with a drink and, still in the barber's chair, quiz his staff on endless lines of prose and poetry he could quote with flair and style.

Congressman Ryan first became aware of People's Temple and Jim Jones through articles that appeared in California papers following the *New West* exposé and from press accounts of the Stoens' custody battle over their son. After he read other news stories—one about an old friend of his, another about a leading defector, Deborah Blakey—his growing concern led to a decision to initiate a full-fledged congressional investigation. He thereby became the only hope for people who had all but given up on receiving help from the government.

One year before the massacre, Robert (Sammy) Houston, who had been an AP photographer for forty years, called Tim Reiterman at the *San Francisco Examiner* and told him that he "was tired of being scared." This resulted in Reiterman's writing an article—a sad narrative of a father's grief over the strange death of his son, Robert, Jr. (Bob), after his involvement and mistreatment in People's Temple. Phyllis Houston, Bob's first wife and mother of their two children, whom Jones directed Bob to divorce, was still devotedly working for and living in the San Francisco church.

After reading the Reiterman article, Leo Ryan contacted Sammy Houston. Bob had been a student of Ryan's in high school, and Ryan had chaperoned Bob and other members of the school band to Washington in 1961, where they had marched in the inaugural parade of President John F. Kennedy. Ryan had especially liked Bob Houston for his keen mind, and he was troubled that such a person could have become a robot for a faith healer like Jones. Moreover, Ryan's nephew had disappeared some years earlier and turned up later in the Scientology cult. Ryan knew firsthand the anguish and fear in the hearts of his own family over a lost child.

The two men, Leo Ryan and Sammy Houston, had happy memories in common—the moment Sammy photographed Bob shaking hands with the new President, and Leo Ryan's proudly leading the high school band past Kennedy's reviewing stand during the inaugural parade. Now they shared dark times. Bob had been beaten, belittled, and berated by Jones; his first marriage had been broken up by the minister; he had worked at two full-time jobs and given everything to People's Temple. His children could visit their grandparents only if they were closely chaperoned by a People's Temple official, Jean Brown, and their mother, Phyllis. They were not even allowed to sit with their grandparents at their father's funeral.

Sammy Houston told Ryan he was dying of cancer and would soon lose his voice. He didn't want to lose his two granddaughters, Judy Lynn, fourteen, and Patricia, thirteen, who had been sent off to Guyana without their relatives. He didn't believe the girls were on vacation, as People's Temple claimed. "They are there without their mother," he said. "I hope my granddaughters will get out of there. I believe they want to get out."

Ryan was a member of Congressman Donald Fraser's subcommittee of the House Foreign Affairs Committee that was investigating the Korean CIA and related activities of another cult leader, Reverend Sun Myung Moon of the Unification Church, and his national and international business enterprises. Although the subcommittee was looking into all facets of United States and Korean relations, Ryan, the idealistic reformer, was interested in only two: why this country was supporting the undemocratic and repressive government of President Park, and Reverend Moon's Unification Church.

Bob Boettcher, staff director of the Fraser subcommittee, periodically briefed the individual members. On one occasion with Boettcher, after a long discussion about the Moonies, Ryan took from his desk a solicitation for mail-order clergymen. He threw it down, saying, "These things are rampant in my district!" and vowed to do something about it.

On June 15, 1978, Marshall Kilduff wrote in the *San Francisco Chronicle* that Deborah (Debbie Blakey) Layton, a recent defector from the Jonestown settlement, charged that the mission was an armed camp in which most people were being held captive. The former financial secretary of People's Temple, she claimed that Jones had "at least ten million dollars" in foreign bank accounts. She also said that people were forced to drink "a bitter brown liquid potion" that they were told would put them to sleep, after which security guards would shoot them.

Jackie Speier, who accompanied Ryan to Guyana, said that Kilduff's article, more than any other, crystallized the Congressman's determination to do something about the people involved with the Temple. They met with Debbie Blakey, and she expanded on what she had told the *Chronicle*. During the White Night drills, the children were forced to drink a liquid and then were told it was poison and they would soon die. On one occasion, Blakey said, she saw her former sister-in-law give John Victor Stoen and her own son, Kimo Prokes, sleeping pills. It seems Jones had told Carolyn Layton that everyone was going to die that night and she would have to kill the two little children, so she felt the sleeping pills would make it easier. Although Speier admitted she had suspicions that Debbie might have been some kind of double agent, Ryan believed her totally. He told Speier, "I smell rats! . . . I'm going to find out for myself."

In the summer of 1978, the Congressman held a meeting with the Concerned Relatives, and after hearing more bizarre stories of human mistreatment, he vowed, "I will go down to Jonestown and see if people are held there against their will." Steven Katsaris, who at first believed that Ryan was just another politician in search of headlines, became more hopeful about him, and Grace Stoen echoed the feelings of the group: "We saw him as someone who was cutting through all the b.s. and was really trying to help us . . . He was the only government person who was sincere." In fact, elections were close at hand. Ryan wanted no one to think he was using the trip for political gain, and did not publicize his decision to go to Jonestown before his reelection in November.

On September 15, 1978, Leo Ryan and Jackie Speier met with the Guyana desk officer and three other State Department officials to make preparations for the visit to Guyana after elections. Ryan informed them of his belief that people in Jonestown were being held against their will and that he would probably be taking members of the press and the Concerned Relatives with him to see for themselves. The State Department "counseled" Ryan against this, but he told them his decision was firm. At the meeting's end, Ryan asked the officials if they were unconcerned about the rumors of mass suicide at Jonestown (as alleged by Blakey); their response was to dismiss such talk as "nonsense."

On October 3, 1978, Richard McCoy, the State Department's consular officer in Guyana, and Richard Belt of the State Department in Washington met with Jackie Speier to discuss details of the trip. McCoy and Belt told her that the American Ambassador to Guyana, John Burke, wanted the Congressman and his staff to understand fully "the difficulties of traveling to Jonestown" and "the need to obtain permission from People's Temple for them to visit the settlement." Speier was upset by the last point, because Ryan did not want People's Temple notified in advance for fear its members would be psychologically intimidated before the actual visit. This fear proved correct.

On October 4, Ryan wrote to the House Foreign Affairs Committee chairman, Representative Clement J. Zablocki, for authorization to investigate. The essence of his appeal was in the following paragraph:

> It has come to my attention that a community of some 1,400 Americans is presently living in Guyana under somewhat bizarre conditions. There is conflicting information regard-

ing whether or not the U.S. citizens are being held there against their will. If you will agree, I would like to travel to Guyana during the week of Nov. 12–18 to review the situation firsthand.

On October 24, Zablocki gave Ryan approval and advised the staff of the committee to assist him.

A few weeks later, Speier and two members of the House Foreign Affairs Committee, Jim Schollaert and Tom Smeeton, informed McCoy that Representative Edward J. Derwinski of Illinois would join Ryan in the congressional inquiry planned for mid-November in Guyana. When Speier told McCoy that the delegation wanted People's Temple to "make available about twenty-nine of its members," including the Stoen child, in Georgetown, the consul vetoed the idea. A few days later, he learned from Speier that eighteen Concerned Relatives would be traveling with Ryan and that they wanted the American Embassy to "arrange transportation and guaranteed access to Jonestown." McCoy said this was impossible but that the State Department would offer suggestions and advice on possible transportation to the area.

On November 1, 1978, Ryan formally confirmed his trip to Guyana with Ambassador Burke and requested the opportunity to inspect the People's Temple Agricultural Community with him and his staff. The same day, Ryan sent Jim Jones the following letter of intent:

> In recent months my office has been visited by constituents who are relatives of members of your church and who expressed anxiety about mothers and fathers, sons and daughters, brothers and sisters who have elected to assist you in the development of your church in Guyana.
>
> I have listened to others who have told me that such concerns are exaggerated. They have been supportive of

your church and your work. Your effort, involving so many Americans from a single U.S. geographic location, is unique. In an effort to be responsive to these constituents with differing perspectives and to learn more about your church and its work, I intend to visit Guyana and talk with appropriate government officials. I do so as a part of my assigned responsibilities as a Member of the House Committee on International Relations. Congressman Ed Derwinski (R-Ill), also a member of the committee, and staff members of the committee will be accompanying me.

While we are in Guyana, I have asked our Ambassador, John Burke, to make arrangements for transportation to visit your church and agricultural station at Jonestown. It goes without saying that I am most interested in a visit to Jonestown, and would appreciate whatever courtesies you can extend to our Congressional delegation.

Please consider this letter to be an open and honest request to you for information about your work which has been the center of your life and purpose for so many years. In the interest of simplifying communications, it will only be necessary for you to respond to Ambassador John R. Burke at the American Embassy in Georgetown. Since the details of our trip are still being arranged, I am sure the Ambassador and his staff will be able to keep you informed.

On November 4, People's Temple representatives told the American Embassy in Georgetown that the "congressional delegation would not be received in Jonestown," but an hour later, they called again and said there had been a misunderstanding and the Ryan party could come if it agreed to three demands:

1. The delegation must have equal representation of people who were sympathetic to the aims of the Temple.
2. There was to be no media coverage with the visit.
3. Attorney Mark Lane must be part of the delegation

in order to represent the interests of People's Temple.

Ryan was told to communicate directly with Lane. In an exchange of letters, Lane informed Ryan that he could not adjust his schedule to accompany the delegation—and asked that they postpone their visit.

In a crisp reply, Ryan told the attorney that a congressional inquiry could not be planned around the schedule of Mark Lane and that they were going regardless. Lane replied with the threat that something very embarrassing could happen to the United States in Guyana, but he quickly "rearranged" his schedule and was in Guyana when the investigating party arrived.

On November 9, the State Department's Legal Adviser's office, in a very strict interpretation of the Privacy Act, informed Ryan that he had "no legal right to demand access to Jonestown."

On the day before Ryan's departure to Guyana, Grace Stoen, Steve Katsaris, and Debbie Blakey visited him in Washington. Their desperate stories of conditions in Jonestown prompted him to call the State Department:

> Look, I've got Debbie Blakey here and you people better talk to her. This is real serious. She is telling me that Jones is making people sell their bodies to get information and is bribing people. I want you to meet with her today.

A half hour later, thirteen State Department officials were willing to meet with the Congressman and his delegation. When Ryan tried to record the encounter, he was told that if there was to be any meeting, he would have to turn off the tape recorder. Debbie Blakey poured out her soul, and the others told everything they knew about the impending crisis. Months later, an in-house evaluation of the State Department's performance said this concerning Blakey's dialogue with the thirteen: "The Department officials were generally impressed with Blakey's story. Some of them were disturbed by the content of her statements." Grace Stoen, however, recalls State Department preoccupation with Ryan's protocol behavior in Georgetown, and the Congressman's reassurance that he would make all the necessary courtesy visits with Guyanese officials and attend cocktail parties and dinners.

It is significant that it was the Embassy in Guyana that notified the State Department as to how many United States journalists were making plans to accompany Ryan, and not vice versa. The source of their information was People's Temple. Jones' network of informers in San Francisco and in the media was still functioning four days before the massacre. Information was transmitted via the Geary Street church to Jonestown. At all times, Jones knew more than the State Department or the American Embassy.

A major source of his intelligence was Tim Carter, the one member of the Concerned Relatives who did not show up for the flight to Georgetown with Ryan and his staff. Carter claimed to be a defector and attended all the meetings of the group, but he relayed everything to Guyana. At one meeting, he learned that Mrs. Robert (Nadyne) Houston and her married daughter, Carol Boyd, were going to try to rescue Mrs. Houston's grandchildren and Mrs. Boyd's nieces, Judy Lynn and Patricia. Carter informed Jones, who ordered their mother, Phyllis Houston, to come immediately and prevent the girls from leaving the settlement. On November 11, Carter and Houston boarded a plane in San Francisco for Guyana, where she would join her daughters in death; authorities would later pick up Carter in the jungle with $500,000 of the People's Temple funds.

On November 14, Leo Ryan, Jackie Speier, and Jim Schollaert of the House Foreign Affairs Committee took an Eastern shuttle flight from Washington to JFK airport in New York. Congressman Edward Derwinski had cancelled his participation in the trip because of a promised weekend with his daughter at college.

The congressional delegation, called CODEL, met thirteen of the Concerned Relatives who were making the trip and eight members of the press at the Pan American World Airways terminal. They boarded Pan Am flight 227, the same flight that had taken many of the children in groups of ten, twenty, and thirty to Guyana the year before—most of them lied to, drugged, or forcefully carried on with their hands tied. The latter happened to Dee Dee Smith, while People's Temple counselors told the airlines personnel she had a "sad history of violent emotional problems."

During the long flight to Guyana, via Trinidad, Leo Ryan talked with each of the Concerned Relatives about their loved ones and prompted questions they wanted him to ask or little things they wanted him to look for in their relatives' personalities to determine if they had been brainwashed.

Their plane touched down at Timehri International Airport, outside Georgetown, Guyana, shortly after midnight, November 15. In the crowd of people, mostly Guyanese, meeting the plane were two Americans— Paula Adams and Linda Sharon Amos, two of Jones' most trusted and loyal lieutenants. (Three days later, on orders from Jones, Amos would slit the throats of her three children, then her own, in Georgetown.)

The Ryan delegation was met by Ambassador Burke's deputy, Richard Dwyer, who was upset because the press had come along. Press members were immediately hassled, and told that their five-day visas had been shortened to one day. All suspected Jim Jones' long arm of political influence.

Ryan had his hands full the first day, trying to straighten out the visa problem for the press and getting the Concerned Relatives in to see the Ambassador. The first evening was reserved for protocol as the Congressman paid a courtesy call on Guyana's Minister of Foreign Affairs, then had cocktails and dinner with the Ambassador. The state-controlled paper, *The Guyana Chronicle*, acknowledged the presence (but not the real purpose) of Ryan's visit to Guyana, reporting that Ryan and the Minister had discussed "the New International Order, the International Commodities, the Sugar Agreement and other topics of world significance."

The Jones propaganda apparatus wasted no time: The People's Temple public relations director at Georgetown, Sharon Amos, handed the Congressman a long scroll with 600 signatures under a petition that read, in part: "Many of us have been visited by friends and relatives. However, we have not invited, nor do we care to see, Congressman Ryan."

On the second day, the Ambassador finally agreed to see the Concerned Relatives for "an hour." The meeting started with a biased slide presentation of Jonestown, which impressed no one who was familiar with how Jones had perfected his public relations scam over the years. But a slide showing Deputy Ambassador Richard Dwyer standing with Jim Jones and his wife startled Ryan and Speier, for it showed him not to be an independent official to whom Jonestown residents could turn if they wanted to leave. After the Concerned Relatives poured out their hearts to Ambassador Burke, he handed them copies of the following statement:

> The People's Temple Community at Jonestown is a group of private American citizens who have chosen to come to Guyana as permanent or semi-permanent residents. As with private American citizens residing anywhere abroad, they

are subject to the laws and the regulations of the host country, in this case Guyana. The American Embassy in Georgetown has no official contact with the People's Temple other than the provision of normal consular services to the individual members of this community on a regular basis. These services include renewal of passports, registration of births, etc. The Embassy has no official authority over the community or its individual members. Except as provided in the Vienna Convention on Consular Relations and in the Bilateral Consular Convention that is in force between our two countries, the Embassy has no authority to require contacts between members of the People's Temple and persons whom they do not wish to receive. The members of the People's Temple are protected by the Privacy Act of 1974, as are all American citizens.

When the meeting was over, many of the relatives broke down and cried. Beverly Oliver called the session "pure bullshit!"

On November 17, Ryan had a heated exchange with Jones' two lawyers, Charles Garry and Mark Lane, in which Garry called the Congressman "a dumb son of a bitch" and stated that he and the delegation weren't going to Jonestown. Ryan let the Ambassador, Lane, and Garry know, in no uncertain terms, that he was going to Jonestown whatever the Embassy or People's Temple thought. He had come to see if people were being held against their will, and come hell or high water, he was going to find out. He gave Lane and Garry two hours to decide if they wanted to accompany him. The lawyers buckled under, and preparations were made to leave for the settlement. Because of seating limitations on the small plane to Port Kaituma, only four Concerned Relatives could make the trip. The group chose Jim Cobb, Beverly Oliver, Carol Boyd (aunt to the Houston girls), and Anthony Katsaris, Maria's brother.

Jones knew from his informer, Tim Carter, that Ryan believed strongly that people were being held in the compound against their will. Carter also told Jones the names of the people Ryan and his delegation wanted to see and why he wanted to meet with them, which meant Jones had plenty of time to coerce, intimidate, and coach those members Ryan and the press would be interviewing. While the investigating body was being delayed in Georgetown by the Ambassador and Garry and Lane, Jones was playing up the fear in his misguided followers. At a mass meeting, Jones threateningly asked, "Who wants to leave with Ryan?" According to Edith Parks, who, after twenty years as a member of the faithful, left with the Congressman: "Jones was telling everyone that 'the Ryan plane will fall from the sky.'"

Jones and his aides believed they could con this visiting group just as they had all the others in the past. Children's toys and the seniors' needlework and crocheting were put on display in the main community hall. There was music and entertainment, and even meat dishes were prepared for the visiting VIPs. For days before Ryan arrived, the young children and older teenagers were coached unmercifully as to what they should say, and were warned of the consequences if they "messed up." The Houston children, who had never read the article about their grandfather's being "scared for too long," were to challenge their aunt, Carol Boyd, on "how unfair the article was to Jim Jones and PT." Everyone was given pat answers to questions that the hierarchy knew the Congressman and his staff would be asking.

On the evening of November 16, while Ryan was dining with the press in Georgetown, a meeting was held in Jones' private quarters, at which the cult leader and his small band of fanatics decided to murder the

Congressman and the press after their visit to Jonestown. Several wanted to do it on their arrival, but the final decision was to see first if they couldn't con the delegation.

Leo Ryan was picked up at the Port Kaituma airstrip and driven to Jonestown before the accompanying press. According to an observer from *The Guyana Chronicle*, Ryan greeted Jones with the list of people he wanted to see and said, "You have been accused of having a totally closed shop where no one can leave." Jones countered that it was all a pack of lies and invited the Congressman to "see what you want to see and talk to whom you want to talk with," adding, "I am sick and tired of all the lies. We have come here to build a peaceful community because it is more comfortable than in San Francisco."

To the outsiders, Jonestown must have been impressive at first glance. A whole community had been hacked out of the jungle and buildings constructed. It was obvious that an enormous amount of time and hard work had gone into the compound. Smiling children played in the playground; infants were lovingly tended in the nursery; cheerful adults went about their baking, laundry, and ground-maintenance chores—all gave the appearance of a very happy existence. Marceline Jones greeted the investigators with a hearty "Welcome to Jonestown" and invited them to a dinner of smoked pork and eddoes—a local root vegetable—potato salad, and coffee, with tarts for dessert.

When the press and Concerned Relatives finally arrived at the compound, thanks to the persistence of Ryan, they were treated with guarded tenseness. Some had not seen their loved ones for more than two years. Outspoken Beverly Oliver was helped from the truck by her two strong sons, William and Bruce. One of the boys leaned close to his mother's ear and whispered, "Mama, please be cool. Things are very, very bad here. Don't say anything, please—we'll talk later."

When the Houston girls saw their aunt, Carol Boyd, they immediately started admonishing her for the *Examiner* article that quoted their grandfather and, according to them, was untrue and unfair to Jim Jones and People's Temple. Maria Katsaris greeted her brother, Anthony, coldly. The Cobb family was detached, if pleasant, to its older brother and son, Jim, whom everyone knew Jones hated fiercely. Cobb was already a marked man: The decision had been made to kill him along with Ryan and certain members of the press.

Congressman Ryan and Jackie Speier set to work immediately, interviewing about one hundred persons, of whom more than half were children and teen-agers. The talks continued during a two-hour show of live musical entertainment. Marceline Jones and Harriet Tropp brought the individuals to Ryan as he requested them. For the most part, he and his staff got pat answers from people with frightened faces. At one point, Speier turned to Ryan and whispered, "There is no question in my mind that there is mind control being exercised here." Ryan agreed, saying the people he was talking with were "unnaturally animated." Both thought the children were "very scared, timid, passive"—only a few were "independent thinkers"—and were giving rehearsed responses. Two young people, Vernon Gosney and Monica Bagby, told the Congressman they wanted out.

Ryan pointed out to Bob Krause of *The Washington Post* how unnatural it seemed for all the old people to be keeping time to hard rock music. He also pointed out a man with a crew cut who appeared to be in his mid-forties: "Look at that man's face, just look at his face!" Both Ryan and Krause saw that the eyes of Tom Kice, Sr., were "glazed." Little did they know that in less than twenty-four hours this man would be standing on the back of a tractor-pulled flatbed trailer, firing a rifle at them.

As the entertainment moved into its second hour, Ryan thought it best to make a few comments to the entire population. He started by saying, "I want to pull no punches. This is a congressional inquiry." He commented further: "I can tell you right now that by the few conversations I've had with some of the folks here already this evening, that there are some people who believe this is the best thing that ever happened in their whole lives." The audience erupted into a twenty-minute standing ovation. To the press, this was the first real sign that something wasn't right. It was clear that People's Temple members were not very sociable. They kept quietly to themselves, shying away from any attempt by the reporters to interview them. They knew only too well that the open walls of the main pavilion allowed the security guards to keep a watchful eye on everything that was said and done.

The press zeroed in on Jones when he showed them the subject of the court custody controversy, John Victor Stoen. Jones told the reporters to see for themselves the striking resemblance between him and the attractive child. "Do you like it here in Jonestown?" Don Harris, NBC correspondent, asked John. The little boy gave a barely audible "yes." When Jones was asked to comment on the allegations of violence, he answered with rancor:

> I do not believe in violence. Violence corrupts. And they say I want power. What kind of power do I have walking down the path talking to my little old seniors? I hate power. I hate money. The only thing I wish now is that I was never born. All I want is peace. I'm not worried about my image. If we could just stop it, stop this fighting. But if we don't, I

don't know what's going to happen to twelve hundred lives here.

At that point, the pavilion lights were turned on and the entertainment stopped, signaling an end to the evening. The arrangement was for Ryan and Speier to spend the night at Jonestown, and the press wanted to as well, but Jones told his wife, "I don't want them here. Get them out of here!" The media left the compound for a late-night bar in Port Kaituma. Ryan and Speier accompanied Richard Dwyer to the Jonestown radio shack, where the Embassy official was keeping in touch with Georgetown. Ryan sent a coded message to Jim Schollaert, who had stayed behind in Georgetown, to order another plane for the next day. Schollaert got the message, which meant some dissidents would be coming out with Ryan.

At the Weekend Discotheque in Port Kaituma, the media people and Concerned Relatives listened to stories of abuse and terror at Jonestown. Hearing that at least two residents per month attempted to escape and there were arms at the camp, the press decided to get tougher with Jones the next morning. Meanwhile, Ryan and Speier decided to split up and interview separately in order to finish up the next day—Saturday, November 18. They also discussed what they would do once they got back to Washington, and agreed that Ryan should not make any statement upon leaving the settlement.

The next morning, after a hearty breakfast of pancakes and bacon, the interviewing began again. Marceline Jones took the press and Concerned Relatives on a special tour of the nursery, the saw mill, the medical facility, the library of 10,000 volumes, and "typical" living quarters. Carol Boyd felt the place "wasn't natural. It was like a summer camp showcase." Some children were baby-sitting their younger peers in the nursery, some were watching videotapes of *Willy Wonka's Chocolate Factory* in the pavilion, and others were engaged in a dance class. While Jones' wife was bragging about how "every Jonestown child was cared for individually," the reporters, annoyed with the control aspect of the tour, started out on their own and discovered one tightly closed building filled with very old people. "The inside resembled a slave ship" was one comment, which even Mark Lane conceded was correct.

Tension built as more and more people asked to get out before it was too late. Dale Parks told Ryan, "We gotta get outa here—this is hell!" His mother, Edith, told Speier she wanted her whole family out, but not to tell Jones until she had gathered them all together. She said that if Jones knew in advance, he would have several family members hidden, making it impossible for all of them to leave. The Parks family ingeniously communicated in a place where no one could talk privately by making believe they were fighting with one another; under their breaths, they passed the word that they were getting out that morning with Ryan.

A very nervous, nail-biting, fifteen-year-old Brenda Parks responded to Jackie Speier's questions for a verbal affidavit:

"What is your wish?"
"I want to go back home."
"Where is home?"
"U.S.A."

After the other members of the Parks family made affidavits, they assembled around Congressman Ryan.

At the same time, Don Harris of NBC was grilling Jones. He asked about the alleged guns in Jonestown. "A boldfaced lie!" retorted Jones. Harris showed the cult leader a slip of paper from Vernon Gosney, asking to leave Jonestown with the Ryan party. Jones grew tense and responded with icy anger: "People play games, friend. They lie. What can I do with liars? Are you people going to leave us? I just beg you, please leave us. Anybody that wants to can get out of here. . . . They come and go all the time." As the interview ended, the newsman shook Jones' hand and said in a friendly voice that he hoped they could meet again. Jones, who had ordered the investigative reporter to be murdered, looked him in the eye and coolly replied: "I shall live in anticipation of that day."

Ryan then approached the minister: "There's a family of six that wants to leave." When Jones saw Edith Parks, his jaw fell. Saying "I feel betrayed," he asked the woman why after all these years she was leaving. Mrs. Parks looked at him steadily and answered with poignancy and courage: "You're not the man I knew." Jones pleaded for sympathy, claiming he had been under a lot of pressure. Still looking him in the eye, Edith replied: "We've been under a lot of pressure, too, and who do you think put us there?" Jones, now almost begging, said quietly, "Don't do this to me, Edith. Wait until the Congressman goes, and I'll give you the money and the passports." With firm resolve, Edith answered, "No. This is our chance. We're going."

But Jones didn't give up easily. During the exchange with Edith, a security guard unobtrusively took twelve-year-old Tracy Parks from the pavilion to a nearby building where Marceline Jones pressed the little girl to stay. Shortly thereafter, Patty Parks (who would be killed at the airstrip) noticed that her daughter was missing and frantically screamed for the child. This emotional scene in front of the Congressman was effective, and Jones motioned a guard to return Tracy.

Ryan had his picture taken with the Houston girls and their aunt, Carol Boyd; then Don Harris interviewed them and their mother. To the reporter's inquiry about their happiness at Jonestown, Judy Lynn replied, "I like it here. I wouldn't want to go back for anything in the world." Her younger sister, Patricia, said she had her passport and could come and go any time she pleased. As was the case with everyone interviewed that day, neither of the girls made eye contact with the camera or the interviewer. Phyllis Houston said she would be leaving Jonestown in a few weeks but felt good that her daughters would be staying in such a safe place. Carol Boyd asked Phyllis when the girls might come home for a visit. "It costs a lot of money to bring them back," she responded.

Harris set up an interview with Bill and Bruce Oliver after their mother, on the advice of her sons, refused one. Bruce Oliver said, "I'm glad Mama and us have some understanding and she understands." What the boys could not tell Harris was that the "understanding" was a planned escape from Jonestown after the departure of the delegation. Mrs. Oliver was leaving money in Georgetown for their flight home.

The Olivers were not the only ones making their own plans to leave Jonestown. Richard Clark and Diane Louie successfully led seven other people out of the compound during the confusion of that morning. It is believed that four other children escaped at this point under the leadership of Joan Salz. The emotional ripples of the Parkses' defection spread throughout the settlement. The climate was visibly volatile. Jones whispered to his trusted bodyguard, Jim McElvane, that he wanted no more defections and ordered him to engineer an incident, if necessary, to prevent anyone else from leaving.

Alvin Harold Simon, a thirty-three-year-old, full-blooded American Pima Indian, had never been an enthusiastic supporter of Jones or the People's Temple. But, like other husbands, he followed his wife, Bonnie Jean, to Guyana because she was fanatically attracted to Jones. She was one of an inner harem, doing whatever Jones commanded. With the Simons were their three children—Alvin Harold, Jr., six; Crystal Michelle, four; and Summer Renee, two—and Alvin's father, Jose, a chief of the Pima tribe. In January 1978, Al Simon had attempted to lead fifty people out of Jonestown, but was unsuccessful and was placed in isolation for his rebellion. Since then, he had been carefully watched.

When Al Simon was spotted approaching Leo Ryan with his three children and his father, a hasty plan was devised. A summons came over the loudspeakers: "Bonnie Simon, please report to the radio shop. Bonnie Simon, please report to the radio shop." There, she was instructed by Carolyn Layton and Jim McElvane to stage the scene designed to cut short the Ryan investigation. NBC captured on film this struggle that was the essence of life in Jonestown. Bonnie Simon screamed, "You bring those children back!" Father and mother tugged at little Alvin Simon, each trying to take him. At the same moment, by prearrangement, Donald Sly pulled out a knife and held it to the throat of Congressman Ryan, saying "You are a motherfucker!"

Lawyers Garry and Lane grabbed Sly and made him drop the kinfe. In the process, Sly cut himself and blood splattered on Ryan. At this point, Dwyer of the State Department ordered the Ryan party to leave, saying he, Lane, and Garry would settle the Simon custody dispute.

Some of the last film footage taken by NBC at Jonestown before the killing began showed Al Simon holding his baby, Summer Renee, in one arm and young Alvin by his other hand, and Jose with Crystal Michelle—all five moving slowly away from the cameras and the pavilion.

Months later, State Department officials told the Pima tribe and the Simon family that Al and Jose did not commit suicide! Poison had been injected into their bodies.

In an eerie scene, the entire Jonestown population silently witnessed the departure of the outsiders and those who were going with them. There was little waving of goodbyes. One last-minute defector, Larry Layton, made the others nervous; they knew how close he was to Jones and suspected Jones had planted him among them. Jim Cobb and the Parkses strongly advised Ryan to watch Layton. As the truck bearing the departers approached the gates of the compound, a young security guard stopped them and searched the vehicle hoping to find his wife and small child, who had escaped that morning. They weren't there, and the truck continued on the muddy road to Port Kaituma.

At the airstrip, Jim Cobb, as he had been doing during the entire trip, again stressed the danger they were in. Ryan said he understood. As the two planes arrived, Ryan announced that six members of the press would have to remain behind until the next day. When told he couldn't leave that day, Bob Krause of *The Washington Post* pleaded with Jim Cobb to give him his seat. Cobb, in an act of courage, gave it to the reporter—in the hope that the world would sooner learn a little more about the place that held his three sisters, brother, and mother in captivity.

The Congressman decided that he would search anyone boarding the larger of the two planes, a de Havilland Otter. Jackie Speier was doing the same at the smaller Cessna. Layton, told he would be flying in the Cessna, insisted he be put in the larger plane. Speier asked Ryan, who told Layton he could get on the larger plane, but only after he had been thoroughly searched. Layton, who had lied to Speier saying he had already been frisked, returned quietly to the smaller craft.

When the tractor pulling the large red flatbed trailer was first seen approaching the airstrip, Don Harris took the cigarette from his mouth and appraised the situation. "Looks like trouble," said the veteran Vietnam War news reporter. Jim Cobb, standing near photographer Greg Robinson, hit the ground when the first shots were fired. After a short lull in the shooting, Cobb reached over to Robinson and said, "Let's get out of here!" But Robinson was already dead. Cobb recognized the Temple members on the flatbed and knew if he stayed there, he was as good as dead. He ran forty yards into the tall jungle grass at the edge of the airstrip.

Patty Parks was just about to enter the larger aircraft when a high-powered shell blew her head open and scattered her brains on the side of the plane. Her daughter Tracy, witnessing the violent death of her mother, froze and screamed hysterically until her older sister grabbed her hand and ran, pulling her into the jungle for safety. Two older children, Tom and Tina Bogue, were already on the plane when Mrs. Parks was hit. They courageously left their seats to close the door, thus keeping the gunmen out of the plane. Both were wounded. Their mother later said: "If those children hadn't shut that door, those gunmen might have gotten on the plane and we'd all be dead now."

One by one, the lethal fire cut down the delegation. Tim Reiterman was hit in the left arm and wrist, Ron Javers in the shoulder, and Bob Krause in the hip. NBC cameraman Bob Brown was struck in the leg while filming the men who were firing. When he fell, one of the assassins walked over and shot him in the face at close range. The NBC soundman was also fired on, but faked death and survived. Don Harris and Leo Ryan hit the dirt behind one of the plane's wheels. Harris fell dead.

Jackie Speier—a "Ryan Girl" campaigner at sixteen and later an intern in Ryan's offices in California and Washington, who went to law school on his advice before becoming his legislative assistant—saw her boss and friend get shot. "Take over, Jackie," he said as he tried to stem the flow of blood from his neck. He was hit again and lost consciousness. Speier, too, was cut down in a blast of gunshots that left four bullets in her body. The gunman walked over to Harris and gave him a coup de grâce, then unloaded their weapons into Ryan's body.

Miraculously, the Cessna took off after Layton was thrown off by Dale Parks. An hour later, it landed in Georgetown, and the Guyanese Armed Forces were notified of the shootings at Port Kaituma.

In Jonestown, the events were under way that would shock the world. Ambassador Burke received a phone call from Prime Minister Burnham, informing him of the shooting at the airstrip. The Prime Minister's reaction to the news was: "Jesus Christ!" John Burke's was a long silence.

Many months later, the House Foreign Affairs Committee would honor the memory of Leo Ryan in Washington with a modest plaque bearing a small stone brought from the airstrip at Port Kaituma and inscribed with Ryan's favorite lines from *Hamlet:*

> Whether 'tis nobler in the mind to suffer
> The slings and arrows of outrageous fortune,
> Or to take arms against a sea of troubles,
> And by opposing end them?

Buses used by Jones to shuttle People's Temple members among the three California churches.

Ukiah, California, People's Temple security guards.

TO WHOM IT MAY CONCERN

I, Timothy Oliver Stoen, hereby acknowledge that in April, 1971, I entreated my beloved pastor, James W. Jones, to sire a child by my wife, Grace Lucy (Grech) Stoen, who had previously, at my insistence, reluctantly but graciously consented thereto. James W. Jones agreed to do so, reluctantly, after I explained that I very much wished to raise a child, but was unable, after extensive attempts, to sire one myself. My reason for requesting James W. Jones to do this is that I wanted my child to be fathered, if not by me, by the most compassionate, honest, and courageous human being the world contains.

The child, John Victor Stoen, was born on January 25, 1972. I am privileged beyond words to have the responsibility for caring for him, and I undertake this task humbly with the steadfast hope that said child will become a devoted follower of Jesus Christ and be instrumental in bringing God's kingdom here on earth, as has been his wonderful natural father.

I declare under penalty of perjury that the foregoing is true and correct.

Timothy Oliver Stoen
Post Office Box 126
Ukiah, California 95482

Dated: February 6, 1972

Witnessed: Marceline M. Jones

Tim Stoen's affidavit attributing the paternity of his son, John Victor Stoen, to Jim Jones.

Jones (left) and John Victor Stoen (right) in Jonestown, the night before the massacre. (*Courtesy NBC News*)

An early photograph of Jones and his wife Marceline (center left) with their natural and adopted children.
(*Courtesy Chicago Sun Times*)

Jones and followers on one of People's Temple's cross-country tours. (*Chicago Sun Times*)

Jones' own "Humanitarian Award," given to key politicians and other supporters of People's Temple. The seal incorporates an outline map of Guyana.

The playground at Jonestown.

Nursery enclosure at Jonestown, as shown to reporters accompanying Congressman Ryan, only hours before the massacre. (*NBC News*)

A dancing class for Jonestown teenagers, the morning of the massacre. (*NBC News*)

Children at the Jonestown reception for Congressman Ryan the night before the massacre. (*NBC News*)

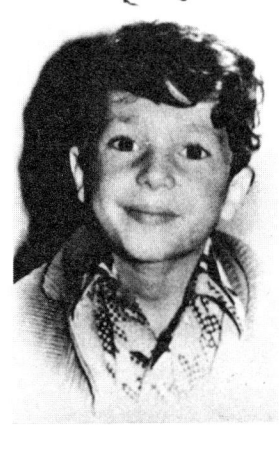
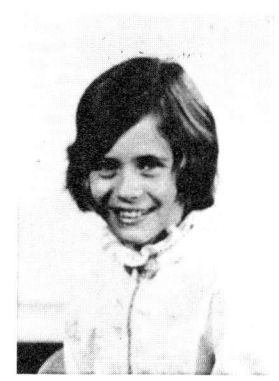

Some of the children of Jonestown—photographs taken from application forms for entry to Guyana. (*Courtesy Ministry of Immigration, Republic of Guyana*)

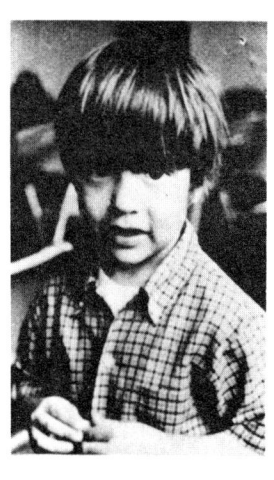
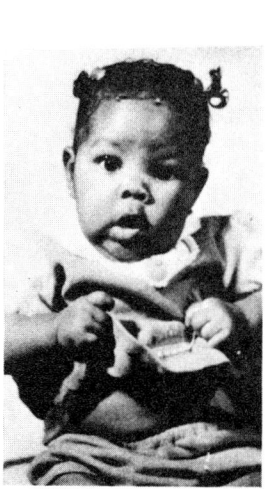
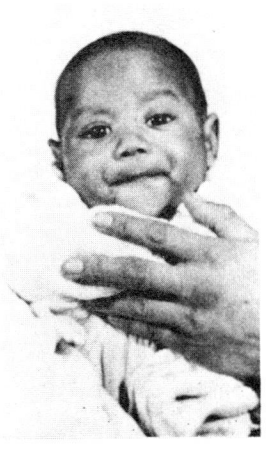

Alvin Simon (left) and Bonnie Simon (center) struggle for their child, Alvin, Jr., moments before Congressman Ryan's departure from Jonestown. (*NBC News*)

Congressman Leo Ryan addressing the people of Jonestown the night before his murder. (*NBC News*)

> *"Silently one by one, in the infinite*
> *meadows of heaven,*
> *Blossomed the lovely stars, the*
> *forget-me-nots of the angels."*
>
> Longfellow, *Evangeline*

9. The Last White Night

The final White Night was the culmination of forty-two previous rehearsals conducted to brainwash approximately a thousand members of People's Temple into preparation for their death. These suicide routines, masterminded by Jim Jones, were precursory to his premeditated act of genocide and would, he hoped, gain him immortality. With the assistance of a few close aides, he executed his plan with atrocious effectiveness. "Jones took those people down there to kill them," said Walter Jones, a former trusted official. "He wanted the world to remember him forever."

Jones may have conceived this mass death as early as the late 1950s, when he read Sara Harris' *Father Divine: Holy Husband.* In the final paragraph of the book, the author wrote:

> If Father Divine were to die, mass suicide among the Negroes in his movement could certainly result. They [sic] would be rooted deep, not alone in Father's relationship with his followers but also in America's relationship with its Negro culture. This would be the shame of America.

When Jones took his followers to visit Father Divine's church in 1972, however, he found that no one had committed suicide after Divine's death. On the contrary, the leader's widow and followers were using his wealth to enjoy the good life on the Main Line of Philadelphia.

It was after Jones returned from this trip and reflected on his fallen mentor that he began to prepare for his own posthumous fame. His plan was to implant the idea of mass death in his faithful and nurture it in his daily haranguings. Shortly after he returned from Philadelphia and the Peace Mission, Jones introduced "Translation" to his "planning commission" (P.C.) counselors—they would take poison with Jones, and after death, the whole group would be "translated to a distant planet to live with him for all eternity."

By 1973, he had begun to sow the seeds of revolutionary suicide in individual members. Grace Stoen recalled a conversation with Jones: "Everyone will die," he said, "except me, of course. I've got to stay back and explain why we did it, for our belief in integration." To teen-ager Linda Myrtle, he preached: "If they ever put me in jail or if I'm killed, we're all to commit suicide, killing the children first, then ourselves."

At times of internal crisis, real or unreal, Jones hammered away at the theme of death for the cause. When Jim Cobb and six other young People's Temple members defected, Jones had his first opportunity to test the other members. Jeannie Mills, in *Six Years With God*, described how Jones handled the situation:

I want to take a vote today to find out how dedicated you all are. Life is a bore. Surely no one here is enamored with his existence. You've seen too much reality in all the hours of counseling at the P.C. meetings. How many of you here today would be willing to take your own lives now to keep the church from being discredited? Perhaps this way we will go down in history as revolutionaries. We could leave a note saying that we were doing this as a sign that we want peace on earth, or that we couldn't exist as an apostolic socialist group, or something like that.

Some of the members indicated they weren't ready to die. Jones wrote down their names and told the group: "The names I have just read are people who can't be trusted yet. A person is not trustworthy until he is fully ready to lay down his life for this Cause." His son-in-law, Mike Cartmell, pointed out that he was willing to do it, but maybe the world would look upon the act as foolish or insane. At this point, Jones dropped the matter.

But the plan was hardly shelved. Jones developed a key theme and drove it home in every kind of communication he held with his people: Individual suicide was wrong, and its punishment extremely harsh—the person would be reborn into the world that existed five thousand years ago. He or she would have to live "five hundred lives" just to get into this century. Revolutionary suicide, however, was on a much higher plane because of the good it would do for humanity. Discussions were held on how to kill everyone on the planning commission. To Debbie Blakey he proposed two ideas—load everyone on a plane and shoot the pilot in midflight, or fill up Temple buses and drive them off the Golden Gate Bridge.

In late 1975, suicide drills—the terrifying "White Nights"—began. First drinks were passed out, then the members were told: "You just drank poison, and in thirty minutes we will all be dead." Guards were stationed at the doors to ensure that no one left. The drills became so frequent that some members of the Alvin Simon family stopped going to the Temple. "Indians do not commit suicide," they said.

Jim Jones knew that San Francisco was not the right setting for his final White Night. Though church members were isolated by indoctrination, communal living, constant surveillance, and armed guards, the purlieus of People's Temple were too fragile, the area too available, for those who wanted to defect. A section of jungle in Guyana was already being cleared and prepared for the ultimate act. He only needed time and a major crisis to provide the rationale for transporting his entire following to the agricultural settlement. Publication of the *New West* article gave him the pretext.

Using his form of biological blackmail, he orchestrated the mass emigration to the small South American country of Guyana. Typical was the example of one-year-old Jakari Wilson, who was shipped out with the first group of children and senior citizens. Her mother, Leslie Wagner Wilson, followed shortly thereafter. Another wave of arrivals brought Leslie's brother and sister, Mark and Michelle. Then Mrs. Inez Jeannette Wagner, their mother, was ordered to Jonestown. When the father discovered what had happened to his children, he obtained a court order for the return of Mark, but as with other Concerned Relatives, his attempt at law and order was short-circuited by Jones.

Guyana was an ideal location, for interference by the law, the news media, or troublesome relatives was practically impossible. Surrounded by thick jungle, Jonestown had only one road leading to it, no telephones, and only a closely guarded shortwave radio. All incoming and outgoing mail was censored, and an intensely loyal, armed security force ringed the community day and night. Upon their arrival, children and adults were trapped. All money, jewelry, valuables, and passports were confiscated. An Embassy cable to the State Department in Washington documented the isolation:

> While we are aware of serious allegations against Jim Jones and People's Temple concerning wrongful appropriation of property, forgery and bodily assaults . . . Department should be aware that it takes a minimum of two to three days to complete such a trip . . . and frequent visits to the area will strain the meager resources of GOG [Government of Guyana].

On November 28, 1977, Temple lawyer Charles Garry quoted Jones as saying "he wasn't sending anyone back." To a local reporter who covered his arrival at Georgetown, Jones said, "I am here with no feeling of a future. Our movement is dead. If I didn't come here . . . we would be destroyed in the U.S.A." To Debbie Touchette, working in the Georgetown office of the Temple, he confided, "We are going down, Debbie; there is no hope."

If anyone managed to escape Jonestown by the single road, which was heavily patrolled and kept in a state of disrepair, or through the snake-infested jungle, the likelihood of getting assistance in a local town or village without money or something to barter was remote. The airstrip was seven miles away, but it was used infrequently, only by charter aircraft from distant Georgetown. Escape by water would have required an eight-hour trip downriver to an ocean port, then a sixteen-hour voyage to Georgetown. The frequent roll calls in Jonestown gave the potential escapee little time to get very far before being overtaken by the armed guards.

Jones bragged that Jonestown was a self-supporting "agricultural mission." But former Temple member Jim Bogue, assigned as farm manager, said the lease Jones signed with the Guyanese government for 3,852 acres of uncleared jungle was only a ruse. The proposal Jones submitted to officials to obtain his lease called for agricultural development of 3,000 acres to support a population of no more than 200 people.

Bogue said it was possible the land might have supported that many people, with strong financial backing from Temple headquarters in San Francisco. But the Temple operation, with its many profitable financial enterprises, was virtually halted after the mass exodus of its members to Jonestown in 1977. By illegally removing children under guardianships from the country, Jones cut off a sizable share of the lucrative Social Security payments he was receiving for the children—another indication that he was burning his bridges behind him. "More than 1,000 people moved to Jonestown that summer," Bogue said. "That was five times what the land would support."

While Jones had always been a meticulous planner, he embarked on his paradise adventure without even testing soil samples at the site. A Guyanese agriculture official said that the earth there was laterite, an extremely acidic red jungle soil from which almost all nutriments had been leached. "There was a curious mismatching of the soil, the technology, and the number of people at Jonestown," he said. Charles Touchette, a former Temple member who helped build Jonestown, said "nothing grew well except the bush and a root vegetable plant." Virtually the only food served at Jonestown was rice, which Touchette brought in by boat from Trinidad. The population, consisting mainly of children and senior citizens whose only farming experience had been that of picking grapes in California, was clearly an inadequate work force. Most of the strong young men and women were made guards and stood in the shade, making sure the others worked ceaselessly.

The original plan for the settlement called for construction of 150 living units. However, only fifty-two had been completed when the big move was made from San Francisco, and Jones ordered Touchette to build no more. This resulted in severe overcrowding. Stanley Clayton said, "The buildings were so crowded that it was almost impossible to dress and undress inside because you kept knocking into other people." There were only two toilets, and for the last four months, one was too full to use. Toilet articles were rationed—one tube of toothpaste per year, one bar of soap per month—and, on Jones' orders, Bibles were to be used for toilet paper.

Guyanese officials who visited the settlement noted that during each tour, the children were always studying the same page, the same lesson. They attempted to place a Guyanese teacher in the compound's school, but Jones reportedly bribed them and threatened mass suicide if the government forced its hand in the matter. He won his case.

Native villagers were extremely impressed with Jonestown's medical unit, and many left the compound with high praise. In reality, however, like everything else, this was for show. Leslie Wilson, who escaped the morning of the final White Night, had become embittered at how the old people were forced to live in conditions reminiscent of a slave ship and hand over their entire Social Security checks to Jones, yet received no medical treatment at all. Even when people were vomiting, they had to continue to work in the fields. Stanley Clayton echoed Wilson's bitterness over the lack of care. "The unit was too busy doping up those who wanted to leave or were critical of Jones or were caught trying to escape, to take care of the sick." The medical unit was one more means of control; in the end, it became the means of death when the medical personnel were turned into killers.

A significant clue to Jones' motivation relates to one of the most expensive pieces of machinery at Jonestown, a huge bulldozer used to clear the jungle. When an inexperienced operator severely damaged the equipment, it cost $100,000 to repair. After that, the only person Jones allowed to operate the machine was Touchette's son, Michael. One day, however, Alvin Simon, in anger and frustration, climbed on it and started uprooting tree stumps. Michael Touchette ran to Jones and told him: "Simon will tear up that bulldozer, and it'll cost us another $100,000 to fix it again." But Jones told Touchette that he was eager to placate Simon at this time. Touchette persisted, but Jones cut him off, saying he did not want Simon to leave; he didn't want anybody to leave.

The security force that Jones developed through total brainwashing and personal favors was as ruthless as any in history and loyal enough to guarantee Jones' appointment with destiny. Leslie Wilson, whose husband was a member, said "Most of them were dedicated enough to kill their own mothers for Jones and the Cause." Headed up by Jones' adopted son, Johnny, the force was armed with shotguns, semiautomatic rifles, and deadly Wham-O-Power-Masters crossbows.

The security guards were better fed than the others and were permitted sex, alcoholic drinks, and other privileges. Most important, they didn't have to work in the fields or perform other hard labor. Their only job was to keep people in the compound and to round up everyone, including the children, to make sure no one left the main area during White Nights. Children who survived Jonestown called them "rough," "mean," and "cruel." Jones had succeeded in expertly playing on the guards' hatred of "the system" and, in many instances, on their incredibly wretched lives before they joined People's Temple, especially in the case of blacks.

Typical of the guards was Marie Duckett, who had been abused as a child, forced into prostitution, and hooked on heroin, and had spent time in prison for felony convictions. Marie was court-ordered into Jones' care; he claimed her as a model example of his successful rehabilitation program: "When someone is rehabilitated in our program, I know it! She [Marie] is one of these." When Stanley Clayton testified at a coroner's inquest after the massacre, he had this to say of Jones' model proselyte: "I walked up to the security to see if maybe I knew one of them and they would let me go. One saw me and jumped back and pulled back her bow and arrow. Her name was Marie Lawrence Duckett."

Having isolated his followers from the outside world, Jones worked on their fears to create a world based on his own imagination. He read the nightly news on the settlement's loudspeakers, warning that frightful danger surrounded them all, that evil men were out there set on destroying their noble experiment. He carefully nurtured the idea that only he could protect his people from the danger that was everywhere, in the jungle and beyond.

One night Stephan Jones saw his father slip into the jungle with a .357 magnum pistol. Shots were heard in the night, then Jones' voice over the loudspeaker announcing a sniper attack.* "He put fear in us to put faith in him," said Michael Touchette.

---

* Stephan told Michael Touchette about similar incidents that occurred while he was growing up in Indianapolis. Stephan said his father would run into the house, shouting that the family was under attack and telling all of them to hide under their beds. Then Jones would run out, and moments later Stephan would hear glass breaking and gunshots. One night he summoned enough courage to look out the window and saw his father standing outside, firing into the air.

For the children, the White Night drills were constant, petrifying nightmares. Many of the drills took place late at night or very early in the morning. Rudely awakened, the children heard the threatening voice of Jones talking about an attack by savage enemies who would cut and dismember their bodies. Many times the security guards forced the youngsters to crawl under the dining-room tent and form walls around it with tables so that they wouldn't be hurt during the attack. Leslie Wilson said the fear instilled in the children controlled every aspect of their lives at Jonestown.

Two months before the final night, Jones ordered everyone to write an "open confessional letter" to him. Eleven-year-old Mark Fields was so caught up in what Jones had been espousing night after night that he wrote:

> If the capitalists came over the hill I'd just drink the potion as fast as I could do it. I wouldn't let the capitalist [sic] get me, but if they did I'd endure it. I would not say a word. I'd take the pain, and when I couldn't stand it any more I'd pass out.

After a delegation of children entreated Jones not to cut off their heads, as he had graphically suggested during one White Night, Jones instructed Dr. Larry Schacht to research the subject of mass suicide by poisoning. On a hot night in May 1978, Jones assembled his followers to see the progress of Schacht's research. Three pigs were brought up from the piggery and injected with syringes filled with different quantities of cyanide. The children, the adults, and Jones watched the ominous results.

More and more drills were carried out. As Debbie Blakey testified in her affidavit: "Because our lives were so wretched anyway, and because we were so afraid to contradict Reverend Jones, the concept [mass suicide] was not challenged." One night everyone, including the children, was forced to drink a strange-looking mixture. The drill ended with Jones saying: "The time is not far off when it will become necessary for us to die by our own hands . . ." As mentioned earlier, he also threatened during this time to kill everyone in a burning building if the courts forced him to return John Victor Stoen to his parents.

According to Stephan Jones, his mother challenged the suicide-by-poison plan. "You can't kill 1,000 people," said Marceline Jones. "There are going to be people [left] alive, brain-damaged. It's going to be a horrible scene." Jones responded that the alternative was torture. At a subsequent meeting of top security personnel and aides, Jones directed Johnny Jones to pick one very trusted person to make sure that after everyone had taken the real poison, no one was left alive. If there were any, they were to be shot.

On Friday, November 17, when the loudspeaker announced, "Alert! Alert! Alert!" Richard Clark instinctively knew he was in extreme danger. From the day he entered Jonestown, Clark had planned to escape, for he hated the compound and he hated Jones. The time was one o'clock in the afternoon, a peculiar hour for a White Night drill. Clark observed that Jim Jones was strangely silent as Marceline announced that Congressman Ryan was coming to the compound. She continued talking in detail for some time and gave everyone instructions. Richard Clark and Leslie Wilson knew by the way "Father" looked that the situation was deteriorating rapidly.

At this point, Jones told everyone to get into good clothes so that they wouldn't look as if they had been working in the fields all day. He also ordered them not to look tired. The gathering broke up with Jones' parting words: "If Ryan gets in, he won't get out alive." As Leslie Wilson would attest later, "Everyone knew something was going to happen to Ryan and that something would greatly affect everyone there." When they left the main pavilion, Richard Clark whispered to his companion, Diane Louie, "Something definitely is going to happen, and I want to be out of here when it does!"

Clark had previously volunteered to help clear the jungle so that he could explore escape routes. He felt certain he knew the way to Matthews Ridge, which was about thirty-six miles from Jonestown. His plan was to take some music tapes with him that he could sell or barter for money to get Diane and himself out of the area. Diane had a close friend in the medical unit, Leslie Wilson, whom she could trust. When told of Clark's plan, Leslie said to count her in, but she also wanted to take her three-year-old child and invite another family, Julius and Sandra Evans and their three children: Sonya, eleven; Sharla, seven; and Shirelle, five.

They decided to leave during the next morning's general confusion and tension of Ryan's interviewing. Diane and Leslie obtained small amounts of Valium and gave it to the younger children so that they wouldn't be frightened or make any noise when the party made its initial move from Jonestown. They left at eight-thirty in the morning and, with much difficulty and determination, arrived at Matthews Ridge at six that evening. Police and army personnel there told them that Ryan had been ambushed, but none of them knew at that moment the people they had left behind were being slaughtered.

Nine escaped in the Clark party; four others are known to have survived once the killing started. The escape parties were small because of the constant vigilance of the security force and because no one knew whom to trust. So effective was Jones in breaking down human relationships, that Leslie Wilson couldn't trust her own brother, mother, or husband. Yet, according to the survivors, more than 90 percent of the people at Jonestown wanted desperately to leave. Sandra Cobb declined to join Leslie because she didn't want to leave her family. She, her mother, and brother Joel wanted to leave but couldn't do it.

In retrospect, there was no logical reason for Jones to kill Ryan and his party. Only a handful of people defected with them. Robert Krause of *The Washington Post* had been very impressed with Jonestown. The NBC interview tapes revealed nothing dramatic except differences of opinion within families. No doubt those who left with Ryan would have told their stories once they were safely in the United States, but Jones and his public relations people had always been adept at neutralizing bad press. Seen in light of this, then, Ryan's murder had only one purpose—to trigger the finale of Jones' self-appointed date with destiny, and cut off the last chance for escape for the children, the elderly, and all the rest.

During the evening of November 17, as the entertaining of the Ryan delegation progressed, Charles Garry felt things were going rather well. Most of the audience felt the same. Yet, for almost no reason, after Leo Ryan praised Jonestown, Jones told the press: "If we could just stop it, stop this fighting. But if we don't, I don't know what's going to happen to twelve hundred lives here."

On the final day, after Ryan, his delegation, and the defectors left the compound for the airstrip, Marceline Jones told everyone to return to his or her cottage and rest while dinner was being prepared in the kitchen. The children were unusually quiet as they intuitively anticipated another White Night. The adults wondered what punishment would be in store for Alvin Simon for attempting to leave with his children and father. Some mothers sensed an even greater and final danger, for they knew the medical staff had been summoned. The following petition was later found crumpled in the mud near Jones' house:

> We, the undersigned mothers, have been shown a dream. We left our homes to follow it. Now we fear that it is about to turn into a nightmare. . . . Dad, we beg of you, don't finally embark upon the step that you have spoken of. Please spare our children. If we must die, let them live. There is nothing noble in dying, nothing fine about killing our children.

But Jones had made his decision. The Ryan party was already under attack at the airport. In a radio message to the forty-six Temple members at Lamaha Gardens in Georgetown, Jones ordered all of them to commit suicide immediately. Lamaha Gardens radioed back that they had nothing available with which to do the deed, and requested instructions. A coded reply said, "KNIFE."

After Liane Harris returned home to Lamaha Gardens from having dinner with her visiting father, Sherwin, at the Pegasus Hotel, her crazed mother cut her throat, as well as her son Mark's and another daughter's. Sharon Amos then cut her own throat, all in blind obedience to "Father." The other People's Temple members in Georgetown disobeyed the order, as did all the followers in San Francisco.

At approximately 5 P.M., Jones' order for everyone to assemble at the main pavilion came over the loudspeakers. Dr. Larry Schacht and nurses Annie Moore and Joyce Touchette finished filling the last of hundreds of syringes with a cyanide-laced sweet drink. The syringes were colored yellow for the infants, rose-pink for the children under ten, and purple for the older children and adults. A box of Magic Markers lay in readiness for the placing of an "X" on infants and children—and eventually on everyone—after the cyanide had been administered.

Security personnel, armed with guns and crossbows, were positioned around the pavilion as the people gathered for the last mass meeting. Stanley Clayton heard security guard Johnny Brown instruct his men over the loudspeakers: "If you see anyone doing a suspicious or a treacherous act—if you see anyone trying to leave—I want them shot."

According to Clayton, Jones then stepped to the microphone and addressed the multitude in fatherly tones: "Let's don't fight one another. Let's do it right. I wouldn't want others to see that we were fighting among ourselves." Once the consequence of resistance had been made perfectly clear to those assembled, a tape recorder was turned on to capture the last moments. However, experts who later examined the tape said that Jones had monitored the recording by turning the machine off and on approximately forty-seven times.

He told his followers the end was near, that the Guyanese Army was preparing to "parachute in here on us. . . . If the children are left, we're going to have them butchered. . . . When they start parachuting out of the air, they'll shoot some of our innocent babies. . . . They've got to shoot me to get through to some of these people. I'm not letting them take your child. Can you let them take your child?"

"No!" said a chorus of voices. "No, no!"

"And I don't think we should sit here and take any more time for our children to be endangered," said Jones, "because if they come after our children and we give them our children, then our children will suffer forever."

A woman, Christine Miller, protested: "I look at all the babies, and I think they deserve to live." Jones countered: "But don't they deserve much more? They deserve peace." Christine continued in protest. "I have the right to choose, and I choose not to commit suicide." At that point, according to eyewitness Clayton, Jones turned off the tape recorder and said, "I'm going to see that you die." Christine Miller, who was not very popular among the people at Jonestown, was baiting Jones to build hostility against her. Ordell Rhodes, impressed with her courage, heard her directly challenge Jones: "Who made this decision for the children? They didn't have any part in this decision. They have a right to life and happiness."

Jones, reportedly furious, kept his temper and replied evenly, "With me dead, nobody would be happy." At this time, the truck pulled in from the airport. Two of the gunmen, Johnny Jones and Tom Kice, jumped from the truck. Young Jones whispered in his father's ear. Jim Jones responded, "We got him—the Congressman—he's dead. Jim Cobb is dead, too." He told his son and Kice to drink the poison. They obeyed and were the first Temple members to die.

The tape recorder was turned on again, and Jones told everyone that the situation was now hopeless and vengeance would swiftly follow. He wanted the 276 children killed first. The children had always been his hostages. He had used them to lure their parents to Guyana and to thwart any plans by the parents to escape. Now the children would serve his final purpose.

With all the flair of a preacher, Jones bellowed: "I want my babies first. Take my babies and children first."

He ordered the poison to be brought to the pavilion. "It's simple," he told the frightened children and their parents. "There's no convulsions with it. It's just simple. Just please get it before it's too late. The G.D.F. [Guyanese Defense Force] will be here. I tell you, get moving, get moving, get moving. Don't be afraid to die. You'll see people land out here. They'll torture some of our children here." On Jones' order, the nurses picked up syringes and began squirting cyanide down the throats of the infants. In some cases, Clayton said, "the nurses plucked babies right out of their mothers' arms" while the mothers stood "frozen with shock, scared out of their wits." When the infants reacted to the potion with piercing, tormented screams, a nurse tried to reassure the crowd: "They're not crying from the pain. It's just a little bitter-tasting. They're not crying out of any pain."

The security guards, using cattle prods, forced mothers to the vat containing the cyanide. Rouletta Paul, who was holding her one-year-old son, Robert, Jr., held her ground and wouldn't move. A guard pressed his gun tightly against her side and said angrily, "You better do it or we're going to shoot your ass off!" The young mother picked up a syringe, shot the liquid down her son's throat, then took some herself. Ordell Rhodes watched as a person standing to one side with a Magic Marker put an "X" on Rouletta. Rouletta walked over to the field, sat down, held her baby to her, and started rocking him.

With the infants dying, Marceline pleaded with Jones to stop killing them. "Mother, Mother, Mother" was recorded before he turned off the tape and confronted his wife. According to eyewitnesses and police reports, an enraged Jones either ordered or pushed Marceline from the table.

"You can't do that to Mother!" protested her personal

bodyguard, Gary Johnson. Jones ordered Johnson to fill a paper cup from the vat and drink it immediately. Johnson acquiesced. Marceline seemed to give up then, and drank the poison herself.

The toddlers and younger children followed the babies to the font of death. Terrified, but not quite understanding what was happening, most of them obediently swallowed the drink. Many of the children who drank at the pavilion went into violent convulsions before they reached the outside area where they were supposed to die, where piles of bodies were being stacked by adult volunteers and security guards. Some died in the men's arms as they were being carried. Others were placed alive on the death piles, face down to hasten asphyxiation. Later, Ordell Rhodes, who had worked with many of these children and was their friend, talked about some of the innocents whom the nurses and security guards brought to him:

> I picked up a pretty little toddler, Tchai Jones. He was shaking so violently with convulsions that I could hardly hold him. His frail little body shuddered horribly. I cradled him tighter in the crazy hope that the force of my hug might somehow keep him alive.
>
> Someone handed me Bippy Romano. She was about six or seven, and God knows how I loved that precious child. She was the kind of kid who could light up your life. It just made your day to see her smile. Now she lay dying in my arms, with her lovely short hair combed so neatly and her beautiful smile erased by a twisted grimace of confusion and pain. My tears wet us both and I hugged her until she died.
>
> I picked up one little girl, Nini Wilhite, whom I had held in my arms just hours earlier. She was a fine, cheerful child, but now her face was a heartbreaking mask of agony. Her eyes rolled up into her head. She gasped for breath and her arms went rigid. Then she was still.

"Many of the children, too, were tricked into taking the poison," said Cecil A. Roberts, deputy police commissioner of Guyana. "They thought it was a game." Cups were handed to boys, ten to twelve years old, who were close friends and usually played and worked together. They ran outside and sat on the ground in scattered groups, facing each other in circles, and drank the liquid. Roberts, a tough cop who thought he had seen everything, said he cannot erase the memory of one cluster of boys, all lying face down in a small circle. "One little fellow was wearing jeans, sneakers, and red socks, and in his back pocket was a slingshot. Just like he came in from playing." Clayton said mild disputes broke out in some families between parents who wanted their children to die with them and children who had been told by Jones that they would only be going to sleep. One of these was an eight-year-old girl who told her mother, "I'm sorry we all have to go to sleep. Can I go to sleep with my friends?" The mother hesitated, then said that would be all right. "Mommy, I love you," said the girl, running off to find her friends. "I love you, too," the mother called after her, tears running down her cheeks.

"Hurry!" Jones shouted to the running children. "Hurry, my children. . . . It's just something to put you to rest. . . . Children, it will not hurt."

As the adults realized that the children were actually dying and suffering terribly, the movement toward the vat came to an abrupt standstill. Jones left his elevated throne, and screaming, began pulling people out of their chairs. The security guards joined him, prodding young people with their weapons. Some began to help force the fatal drink down the throats of the reluctant. Another vat was brought out and placed behind the pavilion.

Jones returned to the microphone and tried to calm the panicked crowd: "I don't care how many screams you hear. I don't care how many anguished cries. . . . Let's be dignified. If you quit telling them [the children] they're dying, if you would also stop some of this nonsense... Adults! Adults! I call on you to stop this nonsense. I call on you to quit exciting your children, when all they're doing is going to a quiet place."

Then it was time for the teen-agers. Some were extremely frightened, in shock, and dutifully lined up and drank the lethal concoction. They knew they had no choice because of the weapons. Force had to be used on the more rebellious ones. A Guyanese youth, fifteen-year-old Jimmy Gill, hid against some rails outside the pavilion. "Security guards grabbed him," Clayton recalled. "There was a struggle. He said, 'OK.' Nurse Annie Moore ran over to him and injected him.... Fred Lewis, fifteen, struggled against taking the poison. They injected him with a needle, too."

Clayton also described the death of Julie Ann Runnels, who, he said, "downright refused to take the poison." She was grabbed and held by Paulette Jackson, her court-appointed guardian, who pulled her head back while Nurse Moore tried to pour the potion into her mouth. The girl spit it out five times. The two women then beat her and again attempted to get the cyanide into her. This time they covered her mouth and nose with their hands so that she could not breathe, forcing her at last to swallow the liquid. Pressured by Jones to "hurry, hurry, hurry!" the nurses and security men injected teen-agers and adults in their backs, necks, foreheads, arms, legs, and sides.

Unpublished Guyanese police photos show the final agony the children endured. Dr. C. Leslie Mootoo, Guyana's chief medical examiner, almost fainted when he first viewed the dead children, who "had pain written all over their faces." One photo shows a teen-age girl clutching a blanket in a death grip; another, a fourteen-year-old girl with her legs pulled upward in a frozen spasm of torment. Other photos are of foaming mouths and noses, and faces covered with hemorrhaged blood. Jones had lied again. It was painful, incredibly painful.

With their children dead or dying, with armed guards all around them, the adults became resigned to their own death. Ordell Rhodes added: "There were people dying right in front of others waiting to get the potion. Some of those waiting looked like they were in a trance. They stood there glassy-eyed, waiting for their turn to die. But others, especially the children, were frightened." It is believed that with all the drugs in Jonestown, the congregation was almost certainly drugged that morning in order to make them less likely to offer physical or mental resistance to the horror unfolding before their eyes.

Shortly before the massacre began, Jones had John Victor Stoen brought to him. With the tape recorder off, he asked the little boy if he wanted to die. John answered, "No, I don't want to die." He was put to sleep and then injected with the cyanide.

It has not been officially determined whether Jones took his own life, but it is certain that it ended with a bullet in the head, killing him instantly. Not for him the poison he forced on the children.

> "Although its features have been barely ruined, it is more horrible than the rest. It is the body of a small child, dressed in a green T-shirt and plaid short pants. The ravages of the poison were unable to remove the innocence of the little girl's face."
>
> Jim Willse, in the *San Francisco Examiner*, two days after Jonestown

10. The Politics of National Shame

George Gallup, Jr., wrote in February 1979:

> The mass suicides and murders in Jonestown, Guyana, were the most widely followed event of 1978, with a remarkable 98% of Americans saying they had heard or read about this tragic occurrence. Few events, in fact, in the entire 43-year history of the Gallup Poll have been known to such a high proportion of the U.S. public.

Yet, despite such widespread national recognition, Nawab Lawrence, Michele Brady, Julie Ann Runnels, and close to 300 other youngsters were neglected and debased in death. High United States officials made decisions ensuring the probability that, of the 276 children murdered (240 under age sixteen), approximately 210 will never be identified.

The Guyanese troops were the first outsiders to reach Jonestown after the final White Night. They entered the compound on Sunday morning, November 19, expecting an ambush, finding instead an eerie silence. The only signs of life were a dog and one old woman, Hyacinth Thrash, who had slept through the entire cult ritual. The incredulous troops quickly left Jonestown with Mrs. Thrash and returned to Georgetown, which was filling up with reporters who had come to cover the death of Congressman Ryan, to give an account of what appeared to be approximately 400 dead people lying in neat rows in the compound.

The body count rose sharply, however, after army and medical officials removed the older children and adults and found, beneath them, the babies and small children who had died first. In many instances, parents had died with their children and appeared to protect them in death. Jones, with ever a mind to public relations, had urged parents to follow their children in death. Security guards had piled mothers and fathers on their children to give the symbolic impression that they wanted to die together. Having divided families in life, Jones had had them reunited in death for show.

The first medical team to arrive at the jungle settlement consisted of Dr. Mootoo and two assistants. Working thirty-two consecutive hours, to the point of prostration from lack of sleep and food, Dr. Mootoo examined, among others, four children: Kawan Carter, two; Yolanda Brown, fifteen; Marcus Anderson, fourteen; and Nawab Lawrence, eleven. Their stomachs contained cyanide and traces of Valium. "The children died from asphyxia due to violent convulsions," said Dr. Mootoo. He also ascertained that at least "eighty-three people had been injected with cyanide." Other tests had to be forgone because of the medical examiner's extreme fatigue and lack of supplies. An American pathologist phoned Dr. Mootoo to offer United States assistance, but Washington never gave permission and denied any knowledge of such an offer.

Dr. Mootoo, who had youngsters of his own, was deeply moved by the children he examined and the conditions he found at Jonestown. He was convinced that had the dinner that had been prepared for both babies and adults been served, the victims would not have suffered the severe pain they did on empty stomachs.

Eleven-year-old Nawab Lawrence stood out in death to Dr. Mootoo and Maurice Dundas, another Guyanese official. Dundas remembered seeing the little boy on his arrival in Georgetown: He wore the same clothes that day as he was wearing on the day of his death. Nawab was born to a heroin addict on November 20, 1967, and hungered for love all his life. In Jonestown, the youngster was "always getting into trouble" and was the subject of sadistic torture and prolonged psychological abuse. Nawab also was the first guardianship case this writer discovered. When the boy was six, a legal brief drafted by Reverend Jim Jones' lawyers stated that Nawab's guardian was "able to offer the minor a positive educational environment in a rural setting."

After a few hours of sleep in one of the compound's buildings, Dr. Mootoo went through the personal possessions left behind in the "slave ships"—the cramped living quarters with twenty-seven bunk beds on each of the two floors. Crowded as they were, the old people, especially, had kept meaningful effects under their mattresses. The medical examiner wearily and sadly read countless letters from relatives in the United States.

Grandchildren wanted telephone numbers in order to call their "grandmom(s) and grandpop(s)," and they wondered why their relatives, so far away in a strange land, didn't write. On the walls were pictures of the writers and hopeful callers—families that Jones had sought to destroy so that each individual's will could be reshaped to obey his demands without question. In fact, it was the bond of the family that finally challenged Jones and made him vulnerable.

It is now known that at least twenty of the unidentified children were Guyanese. A confidential statement given to this author by a Port Kaituma resident who had frequently visited Jonestown said that about fifteen native "mixed" (American/African) children from Arakaka and Mabaruma had been informally adopted by People's Temple. Three children came from Port Kaituma, where their invalid mother still lives. They were David George, seventeen; Philip George, eight; and Grabela George, seven. Two other Guyanese youngsters, named Neil and Derrick, also lived at the commune on a permanent basis. According to former Temple members, a number of native women delivered babies at the Jonestown clinic and left them behind when they went back to their homes. Although these babies were never registered by the American Embassy as American citizens, the following Temple members, among others, informally adopted them: Andra and Tony Walker, Ava Jones (Brown), Sandy Jones, Joyce and Charles Touchette, and Darline Ramsey.

Charles, Michael, and Mickey Touchette and Debbie Blakey concur with the Port Kaituma citizen on the number of native children at Jonestown on that fateful day. A Guyanese source said: "They were all packed up and sent to the U.S.A," with the exception of Jimmy Gill, whose mother, on hearing that her son had been killed while his hands were tied behind him, "ran wild and ran into the bush."

Initially, the United States and Guyana agreed that the 400 known bodies were to be buried at Jonestown. But as the body count rose day by day, so did Prime Minister Burnham's concern that his country would become a cult shrine. He told the U.S. Embassy that the dead Americans had to be removed at once.

The United States military was quickly mobilized and, within several days of Dr. Mootoo's arrival, was on the scene to start the grim task of removing the bodies. The first chore of the troops was to bayonet the bloated bodies to release the internal gases caused by the hot sun and high humidity. The second was more controversial. Although Ordell Rhodes and Stanley Clayton had returned to the compound the first morning to help identify the dead, "on orders from very high up . . . all politically sensitive papers and forms of identification were removed from the corpses." Photos on the cover of *Newsweek* and other magazines and newspapers clearly show that many of the bodies had ID tags on them. Joel Cobb and John Stoen, who are now among the unidentified children, were initially, positively identified. Jim Cobb told *NBC News* in March 1979, "My brother [Johnny Cobb] saw tags on the people's bodies, and only two members of my family have been identified and I want to know why." Lt. Gen. Gordon Sumner later was reported to have said, "It was the first time in [his] military career that [he] saw [his] men politicized." In view of the fact that the order to strip the IDs came from Robert Pastor, of the staff of Zbigniew Brzezinski, President Carter's national security adviser, it is clear that the impulse was to save any possible embarrassment to the Carter administration. This action would, in many cases, make the process of identification impossible for the medical authorities in Guyana and once the bodies had been returned to the United States. Dr. Rudiger Breitenecker, a Baltimore pathologist, said that the seven autopsies at which he assisted "were severely hampered by lack of crucial information which is usually collected in medical-legal investigations." Unaware of the stripping of the bodies and uninformed of Dr. Mootoo's work and findings, the United States pathologists naively told *The New York Times* on February 18, 1979: "We shuddered about the degree of ineptness."

Preparing the children for removal from Jonestown to the United States was no easy task for the GIs assigned to the duty. In fact, the Army and Air Force are quietly providing psychiatric help to many of the young soldiers and airmen who assisted in the removal of the bodies from Jonestown. Sgt. Boy Petrie told the press: "There are a lot of little kids—that's the toughest part. You can tell they are, kinda by the weight of the bags. They just didn't have any choice." Sixty-five were small enough to be placed in 4-foot lockers, and one aluminum coffin held five small bodies. All 913 deceased were sent to Dover Air Force Base in Delaware for identification purposes and final arrangements for burial.

One admitted problem in identifying the children was the deteriorated condition of their bodies. Comparison through pictures was impossible because of body decomposition, and it was also hopeless to try to distinguish races because the pigments bearing skin had peeled off. However, when the bodies arrived at the old Fighter Alert Hangar No. 1315 at Dover, an assembly line was set up, according to Colonel Cowan, deputy director for the Air Force at the Armed Forces Institute of Pathology, and certain characteristics were charted on all the dead: sex, weight, height, and hair color and texture. The FBI took prints of fingers and feet on everyone they could. Dental charting was done and X-rays were taken. Personal effects were photographed with a Polaroid color camera.

When Colonel Cowan was asked if identification could be made on the remaining 210 children, he stated: "It's largely dependent on receiving other dental records . . . an awful lot of them have characteristic dental findings which we have X-rays on. If we had something to compare them to, I'm sure we could identify the people." But later, Cowan made a contradictory comment when he claimed the FBI and the State Department were working hard to come up with new information. "We have exhausted what we have here," he said. "We are at a standstill unless we get new information."

Another reason for the high number of unidentified children is that Guyana never required fingerprinting for anyone under sixteen years of age, and California, where the majority of the children were born, stopped recording footprints in the late 1950s. The practice was stopped, according to the California Bureau of Vital Statistics, because the ink used for the babies' prints came through the birth certificates.

Be that as it may, the remaining fifty-four children born outside California have not had their footprints requested by any United States agency for the purpose of identification. Conrad Banner, head of the FBI's Identification Bureau, allowed that "because of limited resources, [they] were not able to check hospitals and other leads." Although Marvin Sellers was traced to St. Francis Hospital in Trenton, New Jersey, and copies of his footprints were handed over to the FBI by this writer, the Bureau said the quality of the copy was not good enough and the original print was necessary. Mrs. Gaines of St. Francis' Records Department said that because the original prints were on a microfilm with ninety-nine other private records, they would have to be viewed in the hospital's Medical Records Room. Presently, the FBI has still not made any attempt, and Marvin Sellers remains unidentified.

Reaction to the death of the children of Guyana has been largely one of callous disregard. Representative Evans of Delaware balked at the high cost of bringing home the bodies, while Governor DuPont wanted them out of his state as soon as possible. A group of solid San Francisco citizens, including Michael Goldwater, son of Senator Barry Goldwater, voted to send a telegraph protesting the possibility of burying the dead near their "quiet bedroom community." The President of the United States, as well as national and state political leaders, said nothing about this in all of 1979, the International Year of the Child. And, by and large, the religious and civic communities of the nation have also looked the other way.

There are hundreds of youth-oriented groups in this country, especially in Washington, with the express purpose of advocating children's rights. Yet, with one exception, they have been silent on the single most glaring example of denial of human rights for children in several decades. These groups with their vast budgets did not want to risk losing federal dollars, therefore prudently said and did nothing.

In the early autumn of 1979, a Chicago housewife, Kaye Jarrett, decided to organize a national memorial service for the children of Jonestown. Invitations were mailed out to every major child-advocacy organization in the country and to all clergymen in the Capital. Every United States senator and representative received a hand-carried invitation to attend the service and light a candle before the FBI Building to protest the lack of effort on the part of that organization to identify the children. Not one legislator or children's advocate came.

For the 215 or so people who did come to pay their respects to hundreds of murdered innocents, Father Sean McManus of Washington, the only clergyman present, poignantly supplicated:

> Let us pray. Lord, forgive us for not knowing the names of your children, as it is a sign that we really don't know who we ourselves are. May their names be forever before you. May their memory always serve to remind us sinful adults of the crimes we commit against children. Holy Lord and Father, teach the adult world that violence against children is the purest expression of satanic assault on the name of and the person of Jesus.

While a nation, its government, and its agencies ignored the victims, the professionals who had worked closely with the dead, especially with the children, voiced a very different attitude. Dr. Mootoo, who had labored so diligently to give dignity and order to the chaotic death scene, said he almost fainted when he first viewed the youngsters. FBI agents examining the young bodies in Dover thought of their own children and went about their duties with sad attachment. Charles Carson, chief undertaker at Dover Air Force Base during the Vietnam war, said, "I am a father. I have a small boy. That child on that table took on the ID of my child. I had to fight back feelings—anger, love, tears. . . . Those kids didn't make a decision to die . . ." A religious man, Mr. Carson went on to say, "The Lord said, 'Suffer little children and come unto me.'" He tearfully added, "I hope they do."

In February 1979, Judge Ira Brown of the Superior Court of California, who was handling the estate of People's Temple, requested information on the unidentified dead of Jonestown. Carmen A. Diplacido, of the State Department's Citizens' Consular Services, wrote to Judge Brown on February 28:

> Of the 561 bodies remaining at Dover Air Force Base, 253 have yet to be identified. However, with few exceptions, we are aware of the names of the 253 bodies, but in connection with the U.S. Armed Forces Institute of Pathology, in their continuing identification process, we have been unable to match the decedent's name to a certain body among the 253. This, then, is why these decedents are considered as unidentified.

In early May of 1979, roughly six months after their arrival in the United States, a decision was made to bury the children in Oakland, California. Fifty four-foot-long coffins were loaded on a tractor-trailer for a four-day trip across the United States to the West Coast. State Department Attorney Charles Wyman, who was known for his humane attitude to Jonestown relatives across the country, commented on the loading of that truck: "When you see a forklift pick up eighteen boxes and you know they have eighteen children in them, it's got to get to you, unless you're calloused."

Upon its arrival in Oakland, each 20-gauge steel, government-regulation-sized coffin, bearing a coded number to replace the name, was put inside a concrete cemetery liner. Again a forklift tractor picked up the boxes and carried Nawab Lawrence, John Victor Stoen, and their playmates to their final resting place—a huge 50- by 80-foot excavation area that had been dug for all the unidentified bodies. With only a handful of people looking on during that warm, lovely day in May 1979, the neglected, abused, and, finally, murdered children of Jonestown were covered over by the same machine that had carved out the massive hole. Thus did they disappear from the conscience of America.

> *"Not I, not I, but the wind that blows*
> *through me*
> *A fine wind is blowing a new direction of*
> *time.*
> *If only I let it bear me, carry me; if only it*
> *carry me!*
> *If only I am sensitive, subtle, oh, delicate, a*
> *winged gift,*
> *If only, most lovely of all, I yield myself and*
> *am borrowed*
> *By the fine, fine wind that takes its course*
> *Through the chaos of the world. . . ."*
>
> D. H. Lawrence

11. The Cults and Human Rights for Children

Jim Jones, murderer of 276 children and 637 other human beings at Jonestown, left a final mocking message on a board above the throne where he presided over his followers: "Those who do not remember the past are condemned to repeat it."

As a nation, we do not seem to want to remember what happened in Jonestown. Nor do we want to learn how and why it happened. With very few exceptions, Americans, from the President of the United States to people on the street, shrink from discussing the "aberration," an event "too morbid to think about—it's best to forget it." Only Representative Bill Royer, who replaced Leo Ryan in Congress, and newly elected San Francisco District Attorney Arlo E. Smith have persisted in the quest to shed light on the circumstances that culminated in Jonestown. At the local level, Smith has announced his intention to "reopen the investigation into the activation of the People's Temple in San Francisco," while Royer has persistently called on his colleagues to further investigate Jim Jones and his operation.

The demise of the People's Temple membership was a significant, historical event worthy of examination at the level of a Presidential commission. I propose that California name a panel of retired state and federal judges to probe the reason why the Ortiz report, discussed in Chapter 7, and numerous other affidavits and complaints against Jones and his organization were not acted upon. This panel should focus on politicans and bureaucrats, an omission that left the three previous, rather cursory hearings lacking in depth and intent.

When the House Foreign Affairs Committee started their investigation of Leo Ryan's assassination, Chairman Clement J. Zablocki requested the opportunity for his staff to interview Guyanese officials, including the Prime Minister. In an exchange of letters, Guyana responded that such interviews would be feasible if similar questions could be put to Mrs. Jimmy Carter, Vice President Mondale, and other American political leaders who supported Jones in one way or another. Needless to say, nothing came of such a proposal. The political intrigues that gave Jones his power base have yet to be explored.

Without question, the Ethics Committee of the American Bar Association should conduct a professional hearing into the various roles and activities of all People's

Temple attorneys, including Mark Lane, Charles Garry, and Tim Stoen. If our government and the legal profession cannot identify and rectify the causes and means of the injustices done to the children of Jonestown, I call for an inquiry to be instigated by the Secretariat of Amnesty International.

The time has come, too, for in-depth investigations of the other cults that have proliferated in the last decade: the Unification Church ("Moonies"); The Church of Armageddon (the Love Family); the Children of God; Scientology; Foundation Faith Ministries; and The Way, International. While the leaders of these groups may not have Jones' murderous motives, People's Temple was not unique. The methods employed by Jones to manipulate and dominate his disciples are shared by most of these cults today. Followers are coerced into signing over their assets to the "church." Defectors are threatened and harassed while attempts are made to keep control of their children. Brainwashing is used to recruit followers and indoctrinate them. Children are forced to beg on the streets. Key government agencies are infiltrated by cult personnel. Bizarre sexual practices are employed to undermine the bonds uniting families. Threats of costly lawsuits are put forth to intimidate critics and the media, as well as parents who seek to rescue their children. Worst of all, children are routinely neglected, abused, and refused medical attention.

Since the Jonestown massacre, thousands of parents have been organizing against the cults. Their battle, however, is a lonely, uphill struggle against tremendous odds: These quasi-religious organizations are protected by our First Amendment and the government's reluctance to pursue charges of fraud, misappropriation of property, forgery, and widespread child abuse and neglect, perpetrated within the private confines of churches.

Jonestown is not the only place where children have died as a result of fanatical cult ceremonies or at the hands of a lunatic prophet. Cult children have starved in New York, Indianapolis, and Yakima, Washington. Babies born into cults, their births unregistered, are reported to have died of unnatural causes and to have been buried in secrecy, like pets. Does the First Amendment give every "religious" community the license to neglect, abuse, and even murder its children?

Cults thrive on psychological manipulation, but the key to their survival is financial manipulation and, in many cases, financial fraud. At this writing, millions of dollars are being garnered by the new breed of media preachers. Fortunes are being collected through TV and radio solicitations without any accountability being offered to the givers. While the state may not question a cult's beliefs, it should be able to look into its bookkeeping and sources of income. Would it not be a fitting memorial to the Jonestown dead—whose Social Security checks helped Jones build his power base—to require that all religious bodies open their financial records to public scrutiny? Would this violate religious freedom? I don't think so. Taxpayers are entitled to know when the umbrella of "religion" is being used to exploit public funds.

Admittedly, there would be strong opposition from organized religions to such monitoring. Ever since the founding of our country, they have been protected by the First Amendment to the Constitution. Unfortunately, this guaranteed religious freedom has come to be interpreted by churches in its broadest sense, to the point that the rights of taxpayers are being violated. Recently, when a California attorney general investigated the financial records of a very corrupt church, traditional organized religions, particularly the Catholic Church, joined in a chorus of protest. Is the wealth of churches more sacred than the human rights that corrupt ministries jeopardize? Can we not draw the line between religious freedom and vast financial holdings that provide no accounting to the people who labor to bestow on their clergy such immense wealth? What checks are there to keep religion honest? The time to establish them is now.

The House Foreign Affairs Committee's report on Jonestown recommended "inclusion of the subject of cults on the agenda of the White House Conference on the Family" to coincide with the 1981 United Nations International Year of the Family. The report called for a "comprehensive and balanced discussion on the subject of cults, with special reference to their mode of operation, the style and tactics of their leaders, and means and methods by which parents and children can avoid becoming involved with such organizations."

This effort is already being sabotaged by the cults. Much the same as Jim Jones, cult leaders are directing the infiltration of every level of government. Brainwashed as they are to total belief in, and dedication to, their leaders, the infiltrators will let nothing stop them from doing as they are ordered, regardless of what moral or legal issues are involved. We must at least make an effort to better understand and guard against the realities of these multimillion-dollar quasi-religions that trap the youth of our land in their quest for increasing power over lives and fortunes.

To understand the full impact of the tragedy of the children of Jonestown, we must realize that it occurred within the framework of an ongoing and far greater tragedy—the worldwide abuse and neglect of children. In 1978, eight million children died because of misplaced national priorities by various governments. Whereas expenditures of public funds for basic health care, nutrition, and education could have saved untold numbers of children, the world spent $120 billion on new arms. As a result of war and politics, the starving children of Indochina dominated the news in 1979. In 1980, hundreds of thousands of children and their parents became refugees in the wake of the Soviet invasion of Afghanistan. Children, who cannot understand the deadly politics of international leaders and who look to the adult world for protection and safety, are simply left to suffer starvation, illness, and death.

In a report by Ruth Leger Sivard, "World Military and Social Expenditures—1979," the priorities pursued at the expense of the world's youth are documented:

> In the Year of the Child, 8 million children in the world will die as a result of hunger and illnesses related to malnutrition.
>
> Developing nations, with 660 million people who cannot afford the basic necessities of life, spend over $90 billion a year on military power.
>
> The world invests 2,500 times more in the machinery of war than in the machinery of peacekeeping.
>
> In the Year of the Child, 650 million school-age children in the world are not in school.
>
> The strongest military nation in the world has over 25 million people who are malnourished, 10 million children who have never seen a doctor.
>
> In the Year of the Child, the world has added to two of its longest-lived legacies for future generations: a soaring public debt, and a stockpile of nuclear waste which remains dangerous for tens of thousands of years.
>
> In pounds per person, the world has more explosive power than food.

The universality and scale of the neglect and abuse of children might ameliorate the death of 276 youngsters in Jonestown, except for the fact that a free society, governed by just laws, allowed the murder and now chooses to ignore that it happened. The victims of Jim Jones deserve more of a memorial than cold statistics. Would it not be proper for President Carter to award the Freedom Medal, for the first time, to a child? Julie Ann Runnels made such a gallant attempt at life. In spitting out the poison five times as adults held her tight, she embodied the will of all the children to live, even though life was for them hunger, abuse, and terror. I suggest that the President award the Freedom Medal posthumously to Julie Ann on behalf of all the children who were murdered in Guyana. By presenting it at the graveside of these young victims, our leader would not only pay homage to their courage but give them the dignity they deserve.

In the silence of the children's death, the potential of their lives and dreams is haunting. Shawn Valgen Baker, a poet at thirteen, rivaled Langston Hughes in his pride at being black. Ten-year-old Mark Amos was a genius, constantly impressing adults with his creative intelligence. David Chaikin, at fifteen, was a sensitive artist and poet. Denise Boutte and Marvin Sellers wanted to be doctors, and young Ruthie Tupper died with child. Vincent Lopez, Donna Ponts, Joel Cobb, John Victor Stoen, Pattie and Judy Houston, Nawab Lawrence, and hundreds of other children wanted so little and could have given so much.

Candice Cordell was eulogized by a girl friend who survived Jonestown:

> She grew up in P.T. all her life, she didn't know what the outside world was like. And she'd wonder, she'd talk about it, she wanted to know what it was like. "Just for a day," she

said, she'd "like to know how it was on the outside world." It's hard for me to relate to her dying. Because I know she wanted that chance and she never got it. She had no way to get out. Nobody to turn to.

In the final refuse of People's Temple were little dolls, sneakers, baseball mitts, empty Mother Goose shoe boxes, games, assorted toys, and single socks of all sizes. One room was filled with baby cradles, bassinets, a potty chair, and baby bottles. The loss of human potential can never be measured. Those shoes will never be bronzed; the dolls will never again be loved; the sneakers will never wear out at the toes or be covered with dust from play. The toys and games, like the precious lives, are lost to all of us. In a violent world, the gentle words of Pablo Casals attempt to teach us another meaning of the word "proud":

> You may become a Shakespeare, a Michelangelo, a Beethoven. You have the capacity for anything. Yes, you are a marvel. And when you grow up, can you then harm another who is, like you, a marvel? You must cherish one another. You must work—we all must work—to make this world worthy of its children.

Appendix

ACCUSATION OF HUMAN RIGHTS VIOLATIONS BY REV. JAMES WARREN JONES AGAINST OUR CHILDREN AND RELATIVES AT THE PEOPLE'S TEMPLE JUNGLE ENCAMPMENT IN GUYANA, SOUTH AMERICA

TO: *REV. JAMES WARREN JONES*

From: Parents and relatives of children and adults under your control at "Jonestown," Northwest District, Co-operative Republic of Guyana

Date: April 11, 1978

I. INTRODUCTION

We, the undersigned, are the grief-stricken parents and relatives of the hereinafter-designated persons you arranged to be transported to Guyana, South America, at a jungle encampment you call "Jonestown." We are advised there are no telephones or exit roads from Jonestown, and that you now have more than 1,000 U.S. citizens living with you there.

We have allowed nine months to pass since you left the United States in June 1977. Although certain of us knew it would do no good to wait before making a group protest, others of us were willing to wait to see whether you would in fact respect the fundamental freedoms and dignity of our children and family members in Jonestown. Sadly, your conduct over the past year has shown such a flagrant and cruel disregard for human rights that we have no choice as responsible people but to make this public accusation and to demand the immediate elimination of these outrageous abuses.

II. SUMMARY OF VIOLATIONS

We hereby accuse you, Jim Jones, of the following acts violating the human rights of our family members:

1. Making the following threat calculated to cause alarm for the lives of our relatives: "I can say without hesitation that we are devoted to a decision that it is better even to die than to be constantly harassed from one continent to the next."
2. Employing physical intimidation and psychological coercion as part of a mind-programming campaign aimed at destroying family ties, discrediting belief in God, and causing contempt for the United States of America.
3. Prohibiting our relatives from leaving Guyana by confiscating their passports and money and by stationing guards around Jonestown to prevent anyone escaping.
4. Depriving them of their right to privacy, free speech, and freedom of association by:

a. Prohibiting telephone calls;
   b. Prohibiting individual contacts with "outsiders";
   c. Censoring all incoming and outgoing mail;
   d. Extorting silence from relatives in the U.S. by threats to stop all communication;
   e. Preventing our children from seeing us when we travel to Guyana.

The aforesaid conduct by you is a violation of the human rights of our loved ones as guaranteed by Article 55 of the United Nations Charter, and as defined by the Universal Declaration of Human Rights (adopted by the U.N. General Assembly on December 10, 1948). It is also a violation of their constitutional rights as guaranteed by the Constitution of the United States, and as guaranteed by the Constitution of the Cooperative Republic of Guyana (adopted May 26, 1966).

III. THREAT OF DECISION TO DIE

On March 14, 1978, you, Jim Jones, caused to be written on People's Temple stationery a letter "to all U.S. Senators and Members of Congress" complaining of alleged "bureaucratic harassment" and ending with this chilling threat:

> "[I]t is equally evident that people cannot forever be continually harassed and beleaguered by such tactics without seeking alternatives that have been presented. I can say without hesitation that we are devoted to a decision that it is better even to die than to be constantly harassed from one continent to the next."

We know how exact you are in choosing your words, and there is little doubt that this letter was dictated by you personally since it has been your policy over the years to dictate all letters sent to government officials on Temple stationery. Your letter seeks to mask, by the use of irrelevant ideological rhetoric, its real purpose, which is to divert the attention of U.S. Governmental agencies toward your abuses of human rights by putting them on the defensive.

The "1,000 U.S. citizens" you claim to have brought to

Guyana include our beloved relatives who are "devoted to a decision that it is better to die." We frankly do not know if you have become so corrupted by power that you would actually allow a collective "decision" to die, or whether your letter is simply a bluff designed to deter investigations into your practices. There is supporting evidence for our concern in the affidavit of Yolanda Crawford, which shows that you have publicly stated in Guyana that you would rather have your people dead than living in the United States, and that you have solicited people to lay down their lives for your cause. You certainly have been successful in making us fearful as to your intentions.

We hereby give you the opportunity now to publicly repudiate our interpretation of your threat. If you refuse to deny the apparent meaning of your letter, we demand that you immediately answer the following questions:

1. When you refer to "a decision that it is better even to die than to be constantly harrassed," has this "decision" already been made or is it to be made in the future? If made, when and where? Were our relatives consulted? Did anybody dissent? By what moral or legal justification could you possibly make such a decision on behalf of minor children?
2. When you say you are "devoted" to this decision, does it mean it is irreversible? If irreversible, at what point will the alleged "harassment" have gotten so great as to make death "better"? Would it be an International Human Rights Commission investigation, or an on-premise investigation of your operations by the U.S. Government? Who besides you will decide when that point "to die" is reached?

We know your psychological coercion of the residents of Jonestown to be so "totalitarian" that nobody there, including adults, could possibly make such a decision to die freely and voluntarily. The evidence is that our relatives are in fact hostages, and we hereby serve notice that should any harm befall them, we will hold you and People's Temple church responsible and will employ every legal and diplomatic resource to bring you to justice.

IV. MIND-PROGRAMMING AND INTIMIDATION

The affidavit of Steven A. Katsaris is a personal account of his experiences in Guyana. It reveals the terrifying effect of your mind-programming on his daughter, a bright 24-year-old, which has caused her to deny belief in God, to renounce family ties, and to manifest symptoms of sleep-deprivation and a serious personality change.

Yolanda Crawford's affidavit is an eyewitness account of your activities in Guyana by someone present with you. The affidavit shows that you, Jim Jones, preach there the following doctrines: a) that you are God and there is no other God; b) that the United States is the "most evil" nation in the world; c) that allegiance to your cause must replace family loyalty and that parents should be handled at a distance for the sole purposes of collecting inheritances for the cause and of getting them not to cause trouble.

The evidence also shows that you have instituted the following practices in Guyana: a) a centralized chain of command whereby all decisions of significance are to be made by you and, once made, must be followed by Temple members under threat of punishment; b) the stationing of guards around Jonestown to prevent persons from escaping; and c) the use of degrading punishments (for example, eating hot peppers), sleep-deprivation, food-deprivation, hard labor, and other coercive techniques commonly used in mind-programming.

The evidence also shows that you, Jim Jones, confiscate the passports and monies of people upon their arrival in Guyana, prohibit individual contacts with "outsiders," censor incoming and outgoing mail, prohibit telephone calls by Temple members when in Georgetown, and require Temple members to travel in groups. Ms. Crawford's affidavit also shows that you have publicly threatened that anyone who tries to leave the "cause" will be killed.

The aforesaid conduct by you is a wanton violation of the human rights of our loved ones. It is also a violation of their constitutional rights. The physical intimidation is a violation of the penal codes of the United States and the Cooperative Republic of Guyana.

V. THE HUMAN RIGHTS BEING VIOLATED

We hereby bring to your attention, Jim Jones, the particular provisions which guarantee human rights and constitutional rights that you are violating:

1. *Confiscation of Passports.* Your systematic confiscation of passports and all of the monies of Temple members upon their arrival in Guyana is for the purpose of preventing them from leaving and returning to the United States. You are thereby violating Article 13, Section 2, of the Universal Declaration of Human Rights, which reads:

    "Everyone has the right to leave any country, including his own, and to return to his country."

    Your conduct is also a violation of Article 14 (1) of the Constitution of the Cooperative Republic of Guyana, which reads:

    "No person shall be deprived of his freedom of movement, that is to say, the right to move freely throughout Guyana . . . the right to leave Guyana . . ."

2. *Prohibiting Telephone Calls.* You systematically tell all Temple members upon their arrival in Georgetown, Guyana, that they are not permitted, under threat of punishment, to make any telephone calls to family members in the United States or elsewhere, your purpose being to prevent negative information being imparted to relatives in the U.S. Your additional purpose is to overcome the bonds of family which might induce a Temple

member to wish to return to his home in the U.S. This conduct is a violation of Article 19 of the Universal Declaration of Human Rights, which states:

> "Everyone has the right to freedom of opinion and expression; this right includes freedom to hold opinions without interference and to seek, receive and impart information and ideas through any media and regardless of frontiers."

This conduct is also a violation of Article 12 (1) of the Guyana Constitution, which reads:

> "Except with his own consent, no person shall be hindered in the enjoyment of his freedom of expression, that is to say, freedom to hold opinions without interference, freedom to communicate ideas and information without interference and freedom from interference with his correspondence."

3. *Prohibiting Contacts with Outsiders.* You systematically require that all Temple members, while in Georgetown, not communicate or visit with "outsiders" and not leave the communal headquarters (41 Lamaha Gardens) unless in association with other Temple members. You follow the same policy in Jonestown, enforcing your edicts with guards. Your purpose is to prevent anyone going to the U.S. Embassy and causing them to ask questions on how you treat people. Your additional purpose is to discourage Temple members from being exposed to other religions or philosophies, and from viewing their lives independent of communal obligations. Your conduct is a violation of Article 20, Section 2, of the Universal Declaration of Human Rights, which states:

> "No one may be compelled to belong to an association."

It is also a violation of Article 18 of the same Declaration, which states:

> "Everyone has the right to freedom of thought, conscience and religion; this right includes freedom to change his religion or belief, and freedom, either alone or in community with others and in public or private, to manifest his religion or belief in teaching, practice, worship and observance."

Your conduct is also a violation of Article 13 (1) of the Guyana Constitution, which reads:

> "Except with his own consent, no person shall be hindered in the enjoyment of his freedom of assembly and association, that is to say, his right to assemble freely and associate with other persons."

4. *Censoring Mail.* You systematically require that all of the incoming mail and all of the outgoing mail of Temple members be censored by your staff. Your purpose is to discourage negative information being "leaked" to people in the U.S. and to prevent facts about the "outside" world reaching Temple members which are at variance with your "party line." This is shown by the affidavit of Ms. Crawford with respect to the Ku Klux Klan marching in the streets. Because mail is the only means of contact available to our loved ones once they are transported to Jonestown, you have thereby effectively cut off all free expression and correspondence. Your conduct is a violation of the right of our relatives to privacy, family, and correspondence under Article 12 of the Universal Declaration of Human Rights, which states:

> "No one shall be subjected to arbitrary interference with his privacy, family, home, or correspondence. Everyone has the right to the protection of the law against such interference."

Your censoring of mail is also a violation of Article 12 (1) of the Guyana Constitution, which is quoted above.

5. *Extorting Silence From Relatives.* You systematically require that Temple members who write to their family

members in the U.S. threaten in their letters that they will stop all further communication if any criticism is made of you or People's Temple. For example, Donna Ponts is a 15-year-old girl taken to Guyana in July 1977 without her father's knowledge and in violation of a court order requiring her to remain in California unless he gave permission. Attached is a letter from Donna to her grandmother, which starts out saying: "Grandma, hi! How are you doing? I hope you and everyone else are doing good." It ends as follows: "I am sorry to hear that you called the radio station, but since you did, I will not be writing you any more."

Those of us who receive letters from our relatives in Jonestown find them standardized and unresponsive, as if written by machines. But since it is all we have, these letters are very precious to us. You have placed us in the agonizing dilemma of watching helplessly while the rights of our relatives are violated or losing all contact. We have chosen, however, not to yield to your extortion, which is a violation of Article 12 of the Universal Declaration of Human Rights, quoted above, and of Article 13 (1) of the Guyana Constitution, also quoted above.

6. *Prohibiting Our Children From Seeing Us.* Five of the parents who have signed this accusation have traveled from San Francisco some 5,000 miles in order to see their children since you took them to Guyana. The evidence is clear that you have instituted a most pernicious campaign to discredit us in our children's eyes, as can be concluded from the following experiences:

   a. *Steven A. Katsaris.* On September 26, 1977, Steven A. Katsaris arrived in Guyana and attempted to meet with his daughter, Maria. She was prohibited from meeting with him, duress being employed by you to force her to lie to the U.S. Embassy that she did not wish to see her father because "he had molested" her. Mr. Katsaris had with him a letter from Maria, inviting him and saying, "I love you and miss you." On November 3, 1977, Mr. Katsaris returned to Guyana to see his daughter, after first obtaining a promise of assistance from the Guyanese Ambassador to the United States. After days of waiting, Maria was allowed to see her father, but only in the presence of three other Temple members. Maria gave evidence of sleep-deprivation and a behavior pattern extremely hostile and different from that ever manifested before.

b. *Howard and Beverly Oliver.* On December 19, 1977, Howard and Beverly Oliver, together with their attorney, Roger Holmes, arrived in Guyana in order to see their two sons, William S. Oliver (age 17) and Bruce Howard Oliver (age 20). In July 1977 both boys had told their parents they were going to Guyana "for two weeks." The Olivers had a court order from a California Superior Court for the return of William. They also had in their possession letters from each son saying, "I love you." After spending eight days without success trying to see their sons, they were told that "Jim Jones had a council meeting" and the decision was that "it was best that we did not see or talk to our sons."

c. *Timothy and Grace Stoen.* On January 4, 1978, Timothy and Grace Stoen arrived in Guyana in connection with habeas corpus proceedings commenced the preceding August. Although they had a California Superior Court order which ordered you to deliver their six-year-old-child, John Victor Stoen, to them, you refused to let either parent even see their child. The evidence also shows that you have falsely accused Grace as being "unfit" and that on January 18, 1978, three Temple members surrounded Timothy at Timehri Airport in Guyana and threatened his and Grace's lives if they did not drop legal proceedings.

The aforesaid conduct on your part constitutes a violation of Article 12 (1) of the Guyana Constitution, quoted above, and Article 12 of the Universal Declaration of Human Rights, which states as follows:
"No one shall be subjected to arbitrary interference with his . . . family . . ."

VI. DEMANDS FOR RELIEF

We hereby demand that you, Jim Jones, immediately cease and desist from the aforesaid conduct and that you do the following additional acts immediately:

1. Publicly answer our questions regarding your threat of a collective "decision . . . to die," and publicly promise U.S. Secretary of State Cyrus Vance and Guyana Prime Minister Forbes Burnham that you will never encourage or solicit the death of any person at Jonestown, whether individually or collectively, for any reason whatsoever.
2. Remove all guards physically preventing our relatives from leaving Jonestown.
3. Return all passports and money taken from our relatives to them for their permanent possession.
4. Permit and encourage our relatives a one-week visit home, at our expense. (Because our relatives have been in Guyana for months—and some for years—and because it is our belief that they do not know the full People's Temple story and have been prejudiced against their families, we demand you demonstrate in practice your contention that they are their own agents by permitting and encouraging our relatives to visit their families in the United States for one week, with our guarantee that we will provide them with round trip air fare and not interfere with their return at the end of the family visit should they so choose.)
5. Permit our relatives to write letters to whomever they wish, uncensored and in private.
6. Permit our relatives to read letters sent to them in private and without censorship.
7. Abide by the orders of the courts in the United States, which you have heretofore ignored.
8. Notify us within three days on your radio-phone network of your full acceptance and compliance with these demands by contacting: Steven A. Katsaris, Trinity School, 915 West Church Street, Ukiah, California 95482, telephone (707) 462-8721.

Bibliography and Sources

The majority of my sources were personal interviewees, both in Guyana and in the United States. Numerous People's Temple documents cannot be listed for lack of space. They include countless press releases, letters to VIPs, statements of custody, statements of release, power of attorney forms, Social Security lists, letters to pension funds throughout the United States, and brochures.

I was fortunate to work with *NBC News* and sit through many hours of direct interviews with key people and survivors of the tragedy. I made note of that which was relevant to the central issue of the children of Jonestown, as well as of the poignant film shot by the late, courageous NBC cameraman, Bob Brown.

To those whom I have inadvertently failed to give credit, I offer my apologies, and trust they will forgive my human error.

BOOKS

Bugliosi, Vincent, with Curt Gentry, *Helter Skelter*, W. W. Norton & Co., Inc., 1974.

Harris, Sara, *Father Divine: Holy Father*, Doubleday, 1953.

Kearns, Phil, with Doug Wead, *People's Temple—People's Tomb*, Logos International, 1979.

Kilduff, Marshall, and Ron Javers, *The Suicide Cult*, Bantam Books, 1978.

Krause, Charles, *Guyana Massacre*, Berkley Publishing Corp., 1978.

Lane, Mark, *The Strongest Poison*, Hawthorn Books, 1980.

Lifton, Robert Jay, *Thought Reform and the Psychology of Totalism*, W. W. Norton, 1969.

McWilliams, Carey, *Southern California Country—The Cults of California*, Duell, Sloan & Pearce, Inc., 1946.

Mills, Jeannie, *Six Years with God*, A & W Publishers, Inc., 1979.

Nugent, John Peer, *White Night*, Rawson, Wade Publishers, Inc., 1979.

Patrick, Ted, *Let Our Children Go!*, E. P. Dutton & Co., Inc., 1976.

Schein, Edgar, *Coercive Persuasion*, W. W. Norton, 1971.

Thielmann, Bonnie, with Dean Merrill, *The Broken God*, David C. Cook Publishing, 1979.

White, Mel, *Deceived*, Spire Books, 1979.

LEGAL PAPERS

Guardianship of the Person and Estate of Julie Ann Runnels, a Minor, Superior Court of California, County of Mendocino, No. 15959, Substitution of Party in Propria Persona, August 23, 1977.

> *Note:* The above court-appointed guardianship was one of fifty-seven (57) sets of papers found by this author in the People's Temple files. (See Chapter 2.)

James Cobb, Jr., vs. People's Temple of the Disciples of Christ, James Warren Jones (Jim Jones), Teresa Buford, Jean Brown . . . No. 739907. In the Superior Court of the State of California, City and County of San Francisco.

CONGRESSIONAL HEARINGS, WASHINGTON, D.C.

The Assassination of Representative Leo J. Ryan and the Jonestown, Guyana, Tragedy, Committee on Foreign Affairs, U.S. House of Representatives, May 15, 1979.

Examination of the Problems of Abuse and Neglect of Children Residing in Institutions or Group Residential Settings, Subcommittee on Child and Human Development, U.S. Senate, May 31, 1979.

Investigation of Korean/American Relations, Subcommittee on International Organizations, U.S. House of Representatives, October 31, 1978.

The Guyana Tragedy, International Operations Subcommittee of House of Representatives International Relations Committee, February 20 and March 4, 1980.

NEWSPAPERS

Army Times
Catholic Standard (Georgetown, Guyana)
Day Clean (Georgetown, Guyana)
Daily Record (Morristown, New Jersey)
Chicago Sun-Times
The Fayetteville Observer (North Carolina)
The Fayetteville Times (North Carolina)
Guyana Chronicle (Georgetown, Guyana)
National Enquirer
Indianapolis Star (1972 and 1977)
Indianapolis Record (1964)
Los Angeles Times
New York Times (1977, 1978)

San Francisco Chronicle
San Francisco Examiner (Ten-Day Supplement: "Visions of Hell")
San Francisco Progress
Sacramento Bee
Sacramento Union
Philadelphia Bulletin (1965)
Rolling Stone
Sun Reporter (Oakland, California)
Ukiah Daily Journal
Washington Post
Washington Weekly

PROFESSIONAL PERIODICALS

"The Guyana Mass Suicides: Medicolegal Re-evaluation," William J. Curran, M.D., *Medical Intelligence*, p. 1321.
"The Struggle for Wendy Helander," Barbara Grizzuti Harrison, *McCall's*, October 1979.
"The Twisted Roots of Jonestown," Reggie Majors, *Mother Jones*, December 1979.
"The Cult of Death," *Newsweek*, December 4, 1978.
"Jonestown, Survivors' Story," Nora Gallagher, *New York Times Magazine*, November 18, 1979.
"Inside People's Temple," Marshall Kilduff and Phil Tracy, *New West*, August 1977.
"The Seduction of San Francisco," Jeannie Kasindorf, *New West*, December 1979.
"The Making of a Madman," Phil Tracy, *New West*, December 1979.
"Interview with Stephan Jones," *Penthouse*, April 1979.
"Nightmare in Jonestown," *Time*, December 4, 1978.

OFFICIAL AND UNOFFICIAL DOCUMENTS

State Department, Washington, D.C.:

- The Performance of the Department of State and the American Embassy in Georgetown, Guyana, in the

People's Temple Case, by Messrs. John Hugh Crimmins and Stanley S. Carpenter—1979.
- Cable to Secretary of State from American Embassy in Georgetown, Guyana, September 6, 1977; Subject: People's Temple Immigrants (Children).
- Cable to American Embassy from Secretary of State, September 13, 1977; Subject: People's Temple Immigrants (Children).
- Report of the Death of American Citizen Abroad, From the American Embassy, Georgetown, Guyana, April 4, 1979; Subject: Mark H. Gosney, Age 4; Cause of Death: Acute Cyanide Poisoning.
- Letter to Judge Ira A. Brown, Jr., re: Number of Unidentified Dead, February 2, 1979.

Federal Government:

- Placement of Foster Care Children with Members of the People's Temple—U.S. General Accounting Office, May 31, 1979.

State of California:

- Statement by Governor Edmund G. Brown, Jr., Governor of California, *Donahue* Transcript No. 10089, October 8, 1979.
- Investigation Report on People's Temple, California State Department of Social Services, November 1979. Released.
- Special Report by California State Investigator J. C. Ortiz, Case No. DS-050-221-CA, Department of Developmental Services, State of California Health and Welfare Agency, June 6, 1978.

Guyana:

- Notice Papers, Third Parliament of Guyana, First Session, National Assembly; Subject: The Jonestown Tragedy, November 1978.
- Statement by a Guyanese Citizen on Guyanese Children in Jonestown, January 15, 1979, Georgetown, Guyana.

United Nations:
- United Nations Declaration of the Rights of Children, November 20, 1959.

People's Temple:
- Certificate of Amendment of Articles of Incorporation of People's Temple of the Disciples of Christ, June 3, 1974.
- Confidential Attorney/Client Communication—"Projected Offensive Program for the People's Temple," Mark Lane, September 1978.
- People's Temple List of Personnel Who Immigrated to Guyana, December 12, 1978.
- *The People's Forum* (newspaper), March 1977 and August 1977, published by PT.
- Lease and Delegation of Full Responsibility to Operate Business, January 1, 1972. Legal agreement between People's Temple and Richard and Clare Janero to operate Happy Acres and remit public funds to People's Temple.
- Child Abuse Report Against People's Temple, Pomolita Junior High School, October 6, 1975.
- People's Temple Transmission Communications between Jonestown and the church in San Francisco, California:

  Transmission Communication to Jim Jones from James Randolph, Sept. 20, 1977

  Transmission Communication to Carolyn Layton from J. Randolph, Sept. 20, 1977

  Transmission Communication to Debbie Blakey from J. Randolph, Oct. 4, 1977

  Transmission Communication to Jim Jones from J. Randolph, December 31, 1977

  Transmission Communication to Maria Katsaris from J. Randolph, Feb. 12, 1978

  Transmission Communication to Maria Katsaris from J. Randolph, Feb. 14, 1978

  Transmission Communication to Maria Katsaris from J. Randolph, Apr. 11, 1978

- People's Temple Transmission Transcripts: Transmission talk in Spanish from the U.S. to the Jungles of South America attempting International Phone Patch, the Touchette Family, December 3, 1977.
- Tape recording of the final forty-three minutes of the mass deaths at Jonestown, Guyana, November 18, 1978.

Miscellaneous:

- "World Military and Social Expenditures—1979," Ruth Leger Sivard, World Priorities, Leesburg, Virginia.

Index

Abuse, physical, 7–8, 11–14, 67, 71–74
  (*See also* Sexual)
Adams, Paula, 156
Agnos, Art, 107
American Civil Liberties Union, 47, 109
Amos, Linda Sharon, 40, 130, 156, 157, 184
Amos, Mark, 184, 208
Anderson, Marcus, 193
Apostolic Corporation, 78
Armed Forces Institute of Pathology (*see* U. S.)
Arterberry, Tracy, 7

Bagby, Monica, 161, 169
Baker, George (*see* Divine, Father)
Baker, Shawn Valgen, 208
Banks, foreign, 90, 149–150
Banner, Conrad, 198
Beam, Anthony, 13
Beam, Jack, 13, 40
Beck, George Donald, 130
Beethoven, Ludwig van, iii, 209
Begging, children, 79–80, 90, 204
Bell, Griffin, 3–4, 107–108
Belt, Richard, 151
Bible, the, 68, 177
  quoted, 94
Blakey, Deborah (Debbie), 18, 143, 147, 149–150, 151, 154–155, 173, 175, 180–181, 195
Boettcher, Bob, 149
Bogner, Ruby, 10–11, 57, 97
Bogue, Jim, 71, 176

INDEX

Bogue, Juanita, 14, 19, 67
Bogue, Tina, 169
Bogue, Tommy, 8, 169
Bouquet, Clara, 144–145
Boutte, Denise, 208
Boutte, Mark, 87
Boyd, Carol, 155, 158, 159, 161, 163, 165–166
Boynton, Mrs. Wayne, 94
Braden, Bill, vii
Brady, George, 31
Brady, Georgiann, 22, 31–36
Brady, Michaeleen, 36
Brady, Michele, 8, 22, 31–36, 192
Brainwashing (*see* Mind control)
Breitenecker, Rudiger, 197
"Bridget," 90
Broaddus, Arthur B., 32, 33, 120
Brown, Bob, 169, 221
Brown, Edmund G. ("Pat"), 78, 99
Brown, Ira, 200–201
Brown, Jean, 148
Brown, Jerry, 1, 62, 92, 104, 117, 125–127, 128, 129
Brown, Johnny, 185
Brown, Stu, 85
Brown, Willie L., 103, 106, 115
Brown, Yolanda, 193
Brzezinski, Zbigniew, 196
Buckley, Christopher, 22, 27
Buckley, Dorothy Helen, 22, 27
Buford, Terri J., 18, 114
Burke, John R., 140, 151, 152, 153, 156, 157, 159, 170
Burnham, Forbes, 52, 196, 203, 220
  historical comment, 170
Burton, Phil, 140

Caen, Herb, 100, 112
Califano, Joseph, 82
California Bureau of Vital Statistics, 198
California courts, 116–117
  (*See also* Court guardianships)
California Child Abuse Law, 13
California Department of Social Services, 86, 128–129, 135–137
California State Foster Care Association, 36
Callous disregard, 199–200, 201, 207–209
Campbell, Ronald, 22, 26
Caring, importance of, 1–5
Carroll, Ruby, 11, 12
Carson, Charles, 200
Carter, Hodding, 142
Carter, Kawan, 193
Carter, President Jimmy, and administration, 1–5, 17, 62, 104–105, 141, 196, 199, 202, 203, 208
Carter, Rosalyn, 62, 92, 104–105, 141, 203
Carter, Tim, 45, 155, 159
Cartmell, Mike, 172
Cartmell, Patty, 44
Casals, Pablo, iii, 209
Chaikin, David, 116, 208
Chaikin, Eugene, 24, 26, 28, 29, 30, 37, 85–86, 119
  and Brady case, 32–35
Chavez, Cesar, 66
Chicago Sun-Times, vii, 56, 125–127, 128n
Child abuse complaints, 63–64, 127
Children:
  education and teaching of, iii, 2, 207
  rights and needs of, 2, 199, 202–209
  worldwide abuse and neglect of, 206–208
CIA, 70–71, 112, 114, 115
Citizens' Consular Services (State Department), 201
Clark, Richard, 166, 181–182
Clayton, Stanley, 71–72, 177, 179, 185, 186, 190, 196

Cobb, Jim, 38, 41, 49, 55–56, 71, 79, 95, 158, 161, 168, 169, 172, 186, 196
  Cobb family, 38, 55–56
  suit of Jones, 49, 101–102
Cobb, Joel, 183, 196, 208
Cobb, Johnny, 196
Cobb, Sandra, 183
Cobb, Theresa, 81
Colbert, Jackie, 84
Collins, W. Eric, 132
Communal living, 83–84, 85, 89–90
Communist propaganda, 13–14, 70
Concerned Relatives, 7, 50–54, 102, 140, 142, 144, 150, 152, 155, 156, 157–158, 160, 163, 174
Conscience of America, 201, 202–203
Cordell, Barbara, 23
Cordell, Candice, 208–209
Cordell, Richard, 37
Court guardianships, California, 20–37, 79, 117–121, 131
  and move to Guyana, 121–145
  Ortiz report, 130–139
  and parents, 27–28
  breaking up family units, 23–27, 79
  legal manipulations, 21, 24–26
  vulnerable strategy, 29–31
  Brady case, 31–36
Cowan, Colonel, 197–198
Cranston, Alan, 117, 128, 129, 135–137
Crawford, Yolanda, 40–41, 45, 213, 214, 217
Crym, June, 24, 32–34
Cult membership, 60–61, 64–67, 204
Cults, menace of, viii, 4, 148, 149, 196, 204–205
  and financial fraud, 205–206
  and rights of children, 202–209

Cunningham, Millie, 88
Curtis, 74
Curtis, Franklin, 117

Darnes, Najah, 30, 31, 88
Darnes, Ollie, 22, 30, 31
Darnes, Searcy, 22, 30, 31
Davenport, Kathleen, 77
Davis, Angela, 105, 106
Defections, defectors, attempts, 30, 63–64, 80, 92–93, 101–102, 127, 141, 147, 149–150, 166, 167, 172, 174, 177, 181–183, 184, 204
  false, 155, 168–169
Dennis, Eddie, 87
Denny, Dennis, 23, 128, 130
Department of Health, Education and Welfare (HEW), 82, 132
Derian, Patricia, 141, 142
Derwinski, Edward J., 152, 153, 156
Diplacido, Carmen A., 200–201
Disease, 15
Disposal of the dead, 193, 195–201
Divine, Father, 57–64, 68, 69, 99, 172
Donahue (TV talk show), 125–126, 127, 128
Drugs, drugging, 14, 16–18, 70, 74, 98, 138, 144, 177, 191, 194
  drug abuse program, 100, 101, 107
Duckett, Marie Lawrence, 179
Dundas, Maurice, 194
Du Pont, Governor, 199
Dwyer, Richard, 156, 157, 163, 167
Dymally, Mervyn, 62, 104, 105, 133

Einstein, Albert, 106
Elleby, Exie, 29
Ellice, Douglas V., 88, 143

INDEX

Evans, Julius and Sandra, and children, 182
Evans, Representative (Del.), 199

Family Council on Crime Resistance, 94
Family ties, structure, 38–39, 195, 204, 214, 215–219
   breaking, 40–56, 69, 214, 215–219
   investigations of, 50–56
   leaving the country, 47–49
   sexual degradation, 43–46, 204
   techniques, 41–43
Father Divine (*see* Divine)
Father Divine: Holy Husband (Harris), 59, 171–172
FBI, 70, 112, 114, 145, 198–199, 200
Fear, power of, 71, 103, 121, 151, 159, 161, 179–180
Federal Communications Commission, 144
Fields, Mark, 180
First Amendment, 204–205
Fitch, Maureen, 32, 33, 34
Fonda, Jane, 62, 104, 106, 107
"Forever Jones," 74–75
Foster care parents, 23
Fraser, Donald, 149
Freedom Medal, 208
Freitas, Joseph, 62, 103, 105, 112, 140

Gain, Charles, 106
Gaines, Mrs., 198–199
Gallup, George; Gallup Poll, 192
Garry, Charles, 18, 71, 115, 130, 158, 159, 167, 175, 183, 204
Gavin, Steve, 100, 106, 108
General Accounting Office (GAO), California, 117, 128–129, 137–138
Genocide, 4, 171

George, David, Philip and Grabela, 195
Gernandt, Eugenia, 88
Gibson family, 29
Gigg, Stanley, 57
Gill, Jimmie, 190, 195–196
Goldman, Mari, 133
Goldwater, Barry, 199
Goldwater, Michael, 199
Goodlett, Carlton B., 18, 91–92, 99–100, 103, 106, 112, 113
Gosney, Vernon, 89, 161, 164, 169
Government, paralysis and failure of, 116–145
   after the massacre, 192, 194, 196–201
   and move to Guyana, 121–145
   and Ryan's Guyana trip, 156–158
   "Case S," 118–121, 145
   investigations, 117–118, 203
   Ortiz report, 130–139
   stonewalling investigators, 132–134, 139–140
   White House and State Department, 141–145, 151–155, 175
Graham, Robert, 112
Gregory, Dick, 115
Griffith, Mary, 87
Grubbs, Tom, 14
Grunnet, Patricia Lee, 48, 66
Gurvich, Fann, 65
Guyana Chronicle, The, 157, 160
Guyana settlement, situation and character, 174–179
   security force, 178–179
   (*See also* Government; Ryan)
Guyanese children, 195

Haberman, Rhoda, 131
Hall, Joseph E., 107
Happy Acres, 28, 133
Hard Labor, 13–14
Harp, Maxine, 139

INDEX

Harrington, Chuck, 25
Harris, Don, 56, 162, 164–166, 169, 170
Harris, Juanita, 30
Harris, Liane, 142–143, 184
Harris, Sara, 59, 171–172
Harris, Sherwin, 142–143, 184
Hartshorne, Richard, 63
Hayakawa, Senator, 144–145
Hayden, Tom, 62, 104
HEW (*see* Department of Health, Education and Welfare)
Hitler, Adolf, 58
Holmes, Denise, 25
Holmes, Roger, 219
House Foreign Affairs Committee, 82, 88–89, 133, 149, 151–152, 155, 170, 203, 206
Houston, Bob and Joyce, 26
Houston, Judy Lynn and Patricia, 149, 155, 158, 159, 161, 165–166, 208
Houston, Phyllis, 148, 155, 166
Houston, Robert (Sonny), 147–149
Houston, Robert and Nadyne, 49, 155
their grandchildren, 49, 55
Hughes, Langston, 208
Humphrey, Hubert Horatio, 106

Ideals, idealism, 67, 98, 184
Identification of the dead, 192, 196–199
Immortality, Jones's, 74–75, 171–172
"Inside People's Temple" (*New West*), 50
International Year of the Child, 1–2, 4, 199, 207
Investigation, continuing, 203

Jackson, Bernadette, 48
Jackson, Cleave, 25
Jackson, Paulette, 25, 119, 190
James, Ronald, 31

Janero, Richard and Clare, 27, 28
Jarrett, Kaye, 199–200
Javers, Ron, 169
Jesus Christ, 170, 200
JIM-LU-MAR, 77
John Birch Society, 47, 105
Johnson, Gary, 188
Johnson, Joe, 107
Johnson, Rhoda, 66, 70
Johnstone, William S., 32
Jones, Ava, 195
Jones, Jim (James Warren), viii, 2, 4, 9, 10, 28, 193, 208
and abuse of children, 11–19, 67, 72–74, 91, 94–95, 108, 118–121, 130, 194
and custody suit, 18
and mass suicide, 17, 18–19, 49, 51–52, 92, 150, 151, 156, 171–173, 177, 180–181, 211, 212–213, 220
and sexual exploitation, 15–16, 43–46
as God, 57–75, 145, 214
and example of Father Divine, 58–64, 68, 69, 99
brainwashing techniques, 68–75, 159, 161, 171, 179–180, 211, 214–215
coded radio messages, 144, 184
death, 191
decision to murder Ryan, 159–160
destiny and immortality, 74–75, 171–172, 183
destroying the family unit, 39–56, 69, 74, 79, 94, 183, 193, 195, 211, 214, 215–219
and exodus to Guyana, 47–49, 121–124, 176
sued and investigated, 49–56
drug dependence, 16, 18, 70, 138
early history, 59, 77–78
final message, 202

Jones, Jim (James Warren) (*cont.*)
  finances, 6–7, 28–29, 32–36, 40–41, 42–43, 64, 76–90, 93–94, 176, 205
  followers, 64–67, 98
  his nursing homes, 77, 79
  insane terrorist, 6–7, 16, 19, 71
  manipulation of the law, 21–26, 29–30, 36, 83–90, 117
  political influence, 13, 15, 36, 39, 47, 58, 91–115, 203
  (*See also* Public relations)
  response to Ryan's letter, 153–154
  (*See also* Government; Ryan; White Nights)
Jones, Johnny, 178, 181, 186
Jones, Marceline, 41, 43–44, 77, 93, 114, 130, 135, 140, 160, 161, 163–164, 181, 183, 187–188
Jones, Sandy, 195
Jones, Steven, 9, 17, 179, 181
Jones, Tchai, 188
Jones, Walter, 79, 171

Kasindorf, Jeannie, 100
Katsaris, Anthony, 158, 161
Katsaris, Maria, 49, 50, 140–141, 158, 161, 218–219
Katsaris, Steven A., 49, 50, 53, 140–141, 150, 154, 214, 218–219, 220
Kennedy, Grace, 118–121, 145
Kennedy, John F., 148
Kerns, Carol Ann, 87
Kespohl, Janet, 132
Kice, Robert, 87
Kice, Tom, 161–162, 186
Kilduff, Marshall, 50, 108–109, 149–150
King, Martin Luther, 106, 126
Kinsolving, Lester, 108
Kloempken, Rhonda, 36–37
Korean war, 67–68

Krause, Robert, 161–162, 168, 169, 183
Ku Klux Klan, 59, 69, 71, 217

Lacy, Philip, 37
La Guardia, Fiorello, 62
La Mothe, Kenneth, 25
La Mothe, Ramona, 22, 25
Lane, Mark, 111, 113–115, 153–154, 158, 159, 164, 167, 204
Lawrence, D. H., 202
Lawrence, Nawab, 7, 22, 48, 192, 194, 201, 208
Layton, Carolyn, 85–86, 150, 167
Layton, Deborah, 149–150
Layton, Larry, 101, 130, 168–169, 170
Legal Services for Children, Inc., 36
Let Our Children Go (Patrick), 39
Lewis, Freddie L., 76
Lewis, Fred, 190
Lin Wen Hsuen: A Boy Martyr, 13
Lindsay, Gordon, 108, 127
Longfellow, Henry Wadsworth: *Evangeline*, 171
Looman, Carolyn, 30
Loorey, Stuart, vii
Lopez, Vincent, 127, 208
Los Angeles Herald, 103
Los Angeles Times, 94
Louie, Diane, 166, 182
Lowinson, Joyce H., 17
Luther, James W., 119

McCoy, Richard, 88, 122–123, 143, 151, 152
McElvane, Jim, 27, 166, 167
McManus, Sean, 200
Mail, censorship of, 14, 52, 53, 174, 212, 214, 217
Manriquez, Phil, 135–138
Manson, Charles, 58–59
Mao Tse-tung, 106

Marks, Milton, 105
Massacre, investigation of, 124
  (See also Government; White Nights)
Mazor, Joe, 122
Mendelsohn, Robert, 105
Mercer, Henry, 66
Mertle, Al, 30
Mertle, Deanna, 30–31, 43
Michelangelo Buonarotti, iii, 209
Miller, Christine, 186
Mills, A., 30, 40, 72, 144
Mills family, vii–viii
Mills, Jeannie, vii–viii, 10, 12, 20, 25, 30, 40, 43, 67, 72, 81, 144
Mind control, 40–41, 52, 57–75, 159, 161, 179–180, 204, 206, 214–215
  "equality" and "justice," 57, 61, 66–67
  Father Divine's methods, 57–64
  techniques, 68–74
  (See also White Nights)
Mondale, Walter F., 107, 203
Moon, Sun Myung; "Moonies," 149, 204
Moore, Annie, 184, 190
Moore, John V., 112
Mootoo, C. Leslie, 16, 190, 193–196, 197, 200
Moscone, George, 62, 91–92, 103, 105, 140–141
Mueller, Esther, 77
Murdoch, Rupert, 109
Myrtle, Linda, 72–73, 80, 83, 95, 172

National Inquirer, 108
National Newspaper Publishers Association, 99
NBC News, vii, 56, 101, 127, 196
New West Magazine, 47, 50, 100, 108–111, 140, 147, 174
New York Times, The, 17, 197
Newsweek, 196

Oakland *Sun Reporter*, 91, 103, 106, 113–114
  (*See also* Goodlett, Carlton B.)
Obledgo, Mario, 128–129, 130
Office of Human Rights and Humanitarian Affairs, 141
Oliver, Beverly, 158, 160–161, 166, 219
Oliver family, 49, 55, 219
Oliver, William and Bruce, 160–161, 166
Operation Houston, 47–49
Ortiz, J. C.; Ortiz report, 130–139, 203

Panken, Jacob, 63
Park, Chung Hee, 149
Parks, Brenda, 164, 169
Parks, Dale, 17, 164, 170
Parks, Edith, 159, 164–165, 168
Parks, Patty, 165, 169
Parks, Tracy, 6, 70, 165, 169
Pastor, Robert, 196
Patrick, Ted, 39
Paul, Rouletta and Robert, 187
Pension-fund checks, 76, 81
People's Forum, 69, 110
People's Temple, incorporation of, 78–79
People's Temple Choir, 11
Petrie, Boyd, 197
Pettit, Anita, 30
Pettit, Patricia and Paul Anthony, 30–31
Physical abuse (*see* Abuse)
Politics; political influence (*see* Jones, Jim)
Polk, James, 127
Ponts, Don, 49
Ponts, Donna, 55, 208, 218
Privacy Act of 1974, 154, 158
Progress, The (newspaper), 14
Prokes, Kimo, 150
Prokes, Michael, 67, 72, 112
Public relations, Jones's, 89, 91–115, 157, 193

Public relations, Jones's *(cont.)*
  and exploitation of children, 91, 94–95, 97
  collecting the spoils, 97–98, 103
  discrediting critics, 101–102, 109–114
  exposé and examination, 108–114
  hoodwinking the politicians, 92–93, 101, 115
  humanitarian reputation, 92, 93, 99–101, 103–104
  influence peddling, 93–97
  operation in full swing, 99–101
  supporting both sides, 97
  zenith, 103–108
"Public service," 13–14
Purifoy, Bonnie, 83
Purifoy, Denise, 79–80
Purifoy, J. R., 23, 41, 43, 74, 91, 139–140

Radio messages, coded, 144, 184
Ramsey, Darline, 195
Randolph, Jim, 84, 85–86, 130
Reece, Dennis, 88
Reed, Edna, 88
Reiterman, Tim, 148, 169
Religion in American Life, Inc., 103
Religious freedom and corruption, 204–206
Rhodes, Ordell, 186, 187, 188, 191, 196
Richardson, Darwin, 13
Rights of children, 2, 199, 202–209
Roberts, Cecil A., 20, 189
Robinson, Greg, 169
Rockefeller, Nelson, 95–96
Romano, Bippy, 188
Rosas, Kay, 87
Royer, Bill, 203
Runnels, Eddie Jewel, 118, 145
Runnels, Julie Ann, 22, 36, 118–121, 122, 145, 190, 192, 208
Ryan, Leo, 3, 5, 7, 8, 17, 54, 55, 70, 88, 89, 91–92, 101, 124, 125, 137, 146–170, 193, 203
  arranging trip to Guyana, 151–155
  character and early life, 146–147
  in Guyana, 156–168, 181–184
  investigating Jones, 147–151
  letter to Jones, 152–153
  murdered, 169–170

Salz, Joan, 166
San Francisco Chronicle, 100–101, 106, 149–150
San Francisco Examiner, 100, 108, 111, 148, 161, 192
San Francisco Magazine, 109
Sanders, Dorothy, 87
Schacht, Larry, 19, 180, 184
Schollaert, Jim, 152, 155, 163
Schools and children, iii
Schroeder, Debbie, 32, 34
Schweitzer, Albert, 110
Sellers, Alta, 27–28
Sellers, Marvin, 22, 28, 198–199, 208
Sexual exploitation, 15–16, 31, 43–46, 140–141, 204
Shakespeare, William, iii, 209
  Hamlet, 170
Shaw, Joyce, 130
Simon, Alvin Harold, 166–168, 174, 178, 184
Simon, Bonnie Jean, and children, 167–168
Simon, Jose, 167–168
Singing a happy song, 11
Sivard, Ruth Leger, 207
Six Years with God (Mills), viii, 10, 20, 43–44, 172–173
Sly, Donald, 167
Sly, Neva, 71, 73–74

Smeeton, Tom, 152
Smith, Arlo E., 203
Smith, Dee Dee, 156
Smith, Gladys and David, 26–27
Smith, Kelin Kirtas, 22, 26–27
Smith, Robert, 63
Social Security benefits, 76, 77, 78, 81–88, 132–134, 143–144, 176, 177, 205
Souder, Martha, 87
Speier, Jackie, 146–147, 150, 151, 152, 155, 157, 161, 163, 164, 168–170
Starr, Kevin, 108–109
Stoen, Grace, 11, 12, 18, 35, 42n, 46, 49, 50, 54, 72, 81, 102, 130, 147, 150, 154–155, 172, 219
Stoen, John Victor, 18, 46, 49, 50, 140, 147, 150, 152, 162, 181, 191, 196, 201, 208, 219
Stoen, Tim (Timothy Oliver), 18, 23, 24, 46, 49, 50, 53, 67, 90, 102, 103, 119, 140, 147, 204, 219
Stone, Robert, 84–85, 86
Strategy Council on Drug Abuse Prevention, 17
Study, Wayne, Betty, and Bonnie, 143
Suicide and murder, 20, 28, 150, 171–173, 184
(*See also* White Nights)
Summer, Gordon, 196

Talley, Christine, 36
Taylor, Richard G., 139
Taylor, Virginia, 65
Thieriot, Charles de Young, 100–101
Thomas, Lemuel, 87
Thrash, Hyacinth, 193
Touchette, Charles and Mrs., 17, 23, 79, 133, 176–177, 195
Touchette, Joyce, 23, 184, 195

Touchette, Michael, 19, 178, 179, 195
Touchette, Mickey, 49, 54–55, 67, 81, 141, 195
Tracy, Phil, 50, 109
"Translation," 172
Tropp, Harriet, 161
Tropp, Richard D., 65, 95
Truss, Cornelius Lee, 22, 27
Truth Enterprises, 78
Tupper, Janet and Lawrence, 14, 49, 55
Tupper, Ruthie, 208
Turner, Al, 100

Ukiah Daily Journal, 93
United Nations International Year of the Family, 206
Universal Declaration of Human Rights, 51, 215–220
U. S. Agency for International Development, 102
U. S. Armed Forces Institute of Pathology, 197–198, 201

Valley Enterprises, 78
Vance, Cyrus, 2, 52, 142, 220

Wagner, Inez Jeannette and family, 174
Walker, Andra and Tony, 195
Wallach, Robert, 108
Washington Post, 9–10, 161, 168, 183
Wax, Milt, 140
White House Conference on the Family, 206
White Nights, 19, 150, 173–174, 178, 180–181
  last and final, 171, 174, 177, 180, 184–191, 193
  police photographs, 190–191
Wiesel, Elie, 4
Wilhite, Nini, 188

Wilkins, Roy, 106
Willse, Jim, 192
Willy Wonka's Chocolate Factory, 164
Wilsey, Janice, 87
Wilson, Leslie Wagner, 174, 177, 178, 180, 182–183
Wilson, Jakari, 174, 182
Wilson, Jerry, 8
Wings of Deliverance, 77
Wirth, Congressman, 95
Wood, Marilyn, 125–127
Wooden, Kenneth, 125–126, 198
Woods, Marion J., 86, 128–129, 135
"World Military and Social Expenditures—1979" (Sivard), 207
Wright, Guy, 111
Wright, Rosalie Muller, 109
Wyman, Charles, 201

Yasensky, Bruno, 1
Younger, Evelle J., 138–139

Zablocki, Clement J., 82, 151–152, 203

Catalog

If you are interested in a list of fine Paperback books, covering a wide range of subjects and interests, send your name and address, requesting your free catalog, to:

**McGraw-Hill Paperbacks
1221 Avenue of Americas
New York, N.Y. 10020**